Grooming Without Stress!
Safer, Quicker, Happier:

Setting the 21st century grooming table up for success by employing low-stress handling techniques

FOREWORD

In my twenty years of grooming, I've learned many different techniques for handling dogs. Unfortunately, some of the practices still being taught today are out-of-date. In this book we demonstrate that no matter how long you have been working with dogs, you can always improve your handling skills while keeping up with new and current techniques.

Additionally, our desire in writing this book is to give the modern groomer a way to communicate, shape, and teach families about their responsibilities or challenges in performing husbandry procedures on a regular basis with their dogs. The goal is to ensure that the grooming process be comfortable and pleasurable for their animals.

This book takes scientific knowledge and shows how to implement its most modern, effective techniques into your everyday work environment in order to make grooming a stress-free process for both you and the dog. Whether starting out with a young pup or working with an older dog, our book will walk you through procedures step-by-step in introducing all of the techniques that are inherent in the grooming process in order to set you and your clients up for success, and so that you will be empowered to make decisions in the best interests of the pets you groom, and your business. When clients are happy, both human and four-legged, you will see more repeat business and a growing clientele! — Anne Francis, Professional Pet Stylist, Groom Team USA

ABOUT THE AUTHORS

Terrie Hayward holds a Master's Degree in Bilingual Special Education and is a Faculty Member of the Karen Pryor Academy (KPA), a KPA Certified Training Partner (CTP), and a Certified Professional Dog Trainer through the Council of Professional Dog Trainers. In addition, she is a certified Canine Separation Anxiety Trainer (CSAT), an Associate Member of the International Association of Animal Behavior Consultants (IAABC), and a member of the Pet Professional Guild. Terrie has also written articles on training for *BARKS, Pet Business,* and *Grooming Business* magazines, and is the author of the pocket guide to working with deaf dogs, *A Deaf Dog Joins the Family*. (For additional information on how Terrie can assist, go to: positiveanimalwellness.com.)

Jay Andors is a master groomer with almost thirty years of experience working with all breeds of dogs and cats. In the early 1990s, Jay's pit bull, Apollo, developed serious allergies and skin problems. Using his cousin Dr. Robert Loeb's original invention (HydroSurge), Jay personally developed a method of skin debriding—the art of removing dead skin and scabs in order to promote healing—which allowed him to cure Apollo of his constant skin infections. Over the years, Jay has helped hundreds of dogs live better lives as a result of his treatments. Jay attended Brooklyn College and is a graduate of the Karen

Pryor Academy (KPA). He is a KPA Certified Training Partner (CTP) and also a member of the Pet Professional Guild and the Association of Professional Dog Trainers. Jay uses his skills as a groomer, and his knowledge of operant conditioning and positive reinforcement, to shape cooperative behaviors in the grooming salon; he also gives private lessons to guardians in how to develop these behaviors. (Jay can be contacted at perfectbehaviordogtraining.com.)

Anne Francis, Certified Master Groomer, has been a professional pet stylist for over twenty years, joining the team at The Village Groomer & Pet Supply in Walpole, Massachusetts in 1995. The Village Groomer received Best Independent Retail Grooming Salon twice by the Cardinal Crystal Achievement Awards. Anne was the recipient of the Cardinal Crystal Award for Journalist of the Year for her work on the instructional article, "The Grooming Table," in *Grooming Business* magazine. She was a member of Groom Team USA in 2014, 2015, and 2016, finishing in the top five in the last two seasons. Anne has also been recognized for her incredible scissor work, and received the "Taxi Award" at the NEPGP for the best expression and character with a mixed breed. Anne is excited to share the knowledge that she has acquired over the years as she transitions into being an educator in the industry that she loves.

ACKNOWLEDGMENTS

Special thanks to our editor and proofreader, Ellen Andors, for her dedication to this project, and her thorough and meticulous attention to detail while helping to make this book an easy read.

Thank you to Jay Andors for his "light bulb" moment regarding the book's creation and his desire to work to create this resource to help dogs and handlers feel more comfortable with grooming.

Thanks to Mark Hayward and Meredith Orgel for their invaluable assistance with the happy, relaxed cover shot.

TABLE OF CONTENTS

FOREWORD ii
ABOUT THE AUTHORS iv
ACKNOWLEDGMENTS vi
INTRODUCTION 1
1 LOW STRESS GROOMING: How to Get Started 4
2 COMMUNICATION: Body Language, Stress, and Relaxation 11
   Body Language 12
   The fearful dog on the table: The "on and off" game 20
3 CONCEPTS OF DESENSITIZATION AND COUNTER-CONDITIONING .. 23
   Meet and Treat 25
   Reinforcers 27
   Markers 28
   Counter-Conditioning, Desensitization, and the Grooming Process ... 29
4 FIRST IMPRESSIONS 39
   You decide: Choice as a Reinforcer 42
5 THE GROOMING PROCESS 53
   Greeting 53
   Bathing and Drying 56
   Nails 65
   Ear Cleaning 71
6 CHALLENGES AND SCIENCE 77
7 COOPERATIVE CARE 79
   Creating a positive Conditioned Emotional Response (CER) ... 81
   Creating an Aversive Conditioned Emotional Response (CER) ... 83
   Solutions 87
8 MODERN GROOMING PRACTICES 92
   Relationship-Building 92
   Shaping 93
9 SKILLS 100
   Target Training 100
   Stationing 104
   Targeting and Stationing 107
10 TOOLS 109

Blow Dryer	109
The Groomer's Helper	119
Clippers	125

11 SPECIALTY TECHNIQUES: 128
Hand-Stripping and Systematic Desensitization 128

12 SPECIALTY DOGS: Contest Dogs 142

13 FINDING QUALITY PROFESSIONAL GROOMERS AND TRAINERS .147
Finding a Quality Professional Groomer 147
Finding a Quality Professional Trainer 149

14 WORKING WITH PEOPLE 153

REFERENCES 159

INTRODUCTION

Photo credit: Eric Chassey

Helping dogs feel safe and relaxed in the grooming salon is a win-win situation for all—the groomers, the dogs they are working with, and the dogs' family members. That is what we wish to be able to achieve with this book—a comfortable and pleasant grooming experience for everyone—especially the dog.

We discuss how to help dogs get through the grooming process slowly and gently, and how their families can help in this endeavor with home-practice after receiving instruction from the groomer at the shop. This efficient collaboration leads to increased business, higher return and retention rates, a safer working environment, and happier/healthier people and animal clientele.

Basically, we want the dog to feel safe and to feel good about a variety of grooming procedures. This can be done by reducing stress and anxiety with the various science-based methods that we explain step-by-step throughout the book, and that go a long way toward helping groomers be able to work with dogs more efficiently.

We discuss how to first introduce the groomer and the shop to the dog, and the series of steps to help make this a positive meeting. We want to begin by setting the grooming visit up for success! We start from the very beginning, the dog first stepping into the shop—sometimes even before that, outside the front door of the shop.

There are highly detailed and user-friendly step-by-step sample training plans throughout this book for the many different processes involved, some to be shared with families for at-home practice. There are "games" to play to achieve a positive result. There are various methods and procedures explained that can be adjusted for the individual dog.

We hope you enjoy reading and learning from this book as much as we enjoyed writing it and re-learning things along the way!

1 LOW STRESS GROOMING: How to Get Started

Basically, we want the dog to feel safe and to feel good about a variety of experiences.

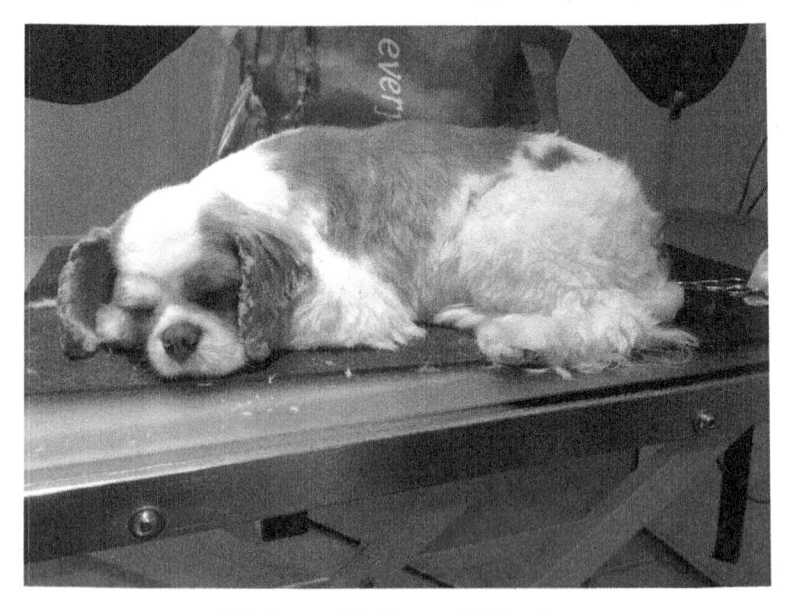

Photo credit: Susan O'Riordan

One important way that we accomplish this is to pair the scary things with good things until the scary things begin to predict good things and we see a change in the dog's conditioned emotional response (CER). We can identify the change in a dog's CER by noting the change in his behavior. Pairing frightening or potentially scary grooming experiences with positive ones is one of the methods we can use in our grooming shops. Doing so helps us to reach our goal of helping animals feel safe, thus setting the stage for easier, more relaxed grooming which, in turn, leads to dogs happily returning again and again; this important concept is discussed in detail in Chapter 3.

First, we want to recognize that if a dog is too fearful to respond appropriately, it will be difficult to train cooperative care behaviors (such as, for example, stationing and lifting foot and/or remaining still for a nail trim).

The way that we begin in this case is to match one "stimulus" with another scenario to change the function of that stimulus (i.e., *pairing*). So, for example, if you are able to successfully pair a stimulus (groomer) having the function of "fear" with a stimulus having the function of "happy yum," you change the function of the scary groomer from "fear" to "happy, yum!!" (Rossman, 2014). Basically what we are saying here is that we want to pair and associate the "groomer" with something the dog likes!

In the past, some harsher methods may have included types of imposing tie-downs and restraints. However, the good news is that today we can accomplish the same grooming goals using gentler methods that do not induce fear or an aversion to grooming. Moreover, these methods produce long-lasting and positive results that are carried over into all the dog's future grooming experiences. Rather than forcibly holding or having multiple people hold down a dog, we can teach a dog to comfortably remain in place and to calmly tolerate, if not enjoy, many grooming procedures. This makes the process faster, easier, safer, and more enjoyable for dog, groomer, and human client alike!

While older techniques and options may work in the short term (the immediate moment), the issue is that there is a heavy price to pay when using such tactics. The big picture is that we may end up with a dog having great anxiety about the grooming experience in general. Moreover, the dog has learned, via this one experience, that the grooming shop is a place where it may feel very uncomfortable and frightened. As such, it is very important to understand that shaping a relationship of cooperation between your animal and the groomer—right at the beginning—goes a long way in teaching your dog to generalize the idea of cooperation and trust.

This fostering cooperation is a team effort! Thus, it is very important for the whole team—in this case, the animal, the family, and the groomer—to be on the same page about helping the dog feel comfortable about the grooming process. This is a great opportunity to build a lasting, long-term relationship along with positive grooming behaviors.

According to Ken Ramirez (Executive V.P. and Chief Training Officer of Karen Pryor Clicker Training, and forty-year respected veteran of animal care and training), behaviors that may be perceived as uncomfortable should be built slowly and over time. Since grooming is a reoccurring event in the animal's life, involving many potentially uncomfortable behaviors, building a positive association in this manner should be an important consideration when going through the process step-by-step. (Side benefit: The time spent patiently teaching the guardian and dog the necessary principles of desensitization and counter-conditioning can also earn the groomer additional income!)

This way, the guardian is a partner in the process, and the team approach allows for us to more effectively teach the animal to accept and feel comfortable with certain experiences that might otherwise be frightening and uncomfortable. This is accomplished by creating a strong, positive history of reinforcement that pairs uncomfortable experiences with positive ones as the dog learns to remain still and calm.

This book endeavors to offer ways to develop a relationship of respect, cooperation and trust by teaching the animal those behaviors that allow for a safer, healthier, and more enjoyable grooming relationship.

If, at any time throughout a process, the dog won't accept high-value treats, this should provide you with information about the dog's fear and anxiety level. A dog that is uninterested in high-value treats is indicative of an anorexic dog or a dog whose stress level is over threshold. If this were to happen, the choice comes down to whether to continue and get the job done as fast as possible, or to stop and take a break. We highly recommend that you take a break and do not "force" the dog to continue. It is scientifically proven that while you might accomplish the groom, forging ahead will only make the fearfulness exponentially worse the next time, which, ultimately, makes for a longer, more dangerous process in the future.

Ideally, building a relationship with the guardians, such that you can suggest and they will heed your recommendation(s), is key. Recommending that they bring their dog back when he's more relaxed in order to finish the grooming process would be the best option in this scenario. This would help you be able to proceed at a pace that the dog could comfortably accept, and would let you shape the behavior in a non-threatening (to the dog) manner. The guardian should wait at least a day or two before coming back to the shop so that the dog has a chance to calm down.

Photo credit: Beth Farrell

In the case of a matted dog, rather than trying to de-matt a stressed dog, consider the alternative of shaving down the dog, at least the first time. Often, a dog that is highly stressed by going to the groomer's is most likely matted as a result of not having kept up with regular grooming visits. Explain to the guardian that your professional recommendation is to shave down the dog for this first time in order to create the least amount of stress while you then start to build a relationship of cooperation. The alternative—de-matting—would only serve to increase the stress, and cause exponentially more anxiety at the next grooming visit. Besides helping the dog, you can think of this as a way to earn more income and to shape a better relationship with the dog's family!

There are many opportunities for this relationship-building during the grooming process. As such, we have outlined a number of sample grooming procedures that can serve as guides. For many dogs, grooming is often a stressful and anxiety provoking situation. It is our goal to work toward collaboratively helping the dog to feel more relaxed and calm with the grooming shop, its procedures, and the groomer.

2 COMMUNICATION: Body Language, Stress, and Relaxation

Let's begin by talking about stress and how it is defined. According to the Merriam-Webster definition: "Stress is a state of mental tension and worry caused by problems in your life, work, etc.; something that causes strong feelings of worry or anxiety."

For our purposes, let's discuss how this applies to dogs. Stress is a state resulting from bodily or mental tensions that tend to alter an existing equilibrium. By learning to observe the dog's body language, we can recognize how the dog is feeling at that particular moment and take proactive steps to avoid his stress acceleration by adapting and adjusting the way we groom that specific dog on that particular day.

Many times, well-meaning groomers, upon noting a nervous or obviously stressed dog, do just the opposite of what is in the dog's best interests: they will frequently pick the dog up and hug it, as one might do when consoling or comforting a child. The issue here is that dogs generally don't like to be hugged, and certainly, when stressed, often don't appreciate this type of attention from a stranger.

It is these well-intentioned but ill-informed behaviors that we'd like to help you adjust in order to recognize, address, and/or approach differently, for a more relaxed and happy grooming visit.

Body Language

Dogs are very obvious in their displays of body language. All their signs of stress come automatically from an internal state. One of the objectives of this book is to teach groomers how to observe, interpret, and better understand canine body language.

Photo credit: Anne Francis

Groomers can envision beforehand how a dog will look after the cut is done, having seen so many before-and-after cuts of a great many dogs in their shops. Groomers are already good observers! With some additional coaching, groomers can learn how to improve upon verbalizing and characterizing what they see in terms of canine body language. That is, we are here to help groomers further refine their observation skills into keen interpretation of body language.

Relaxation

What do dogs look like when they are relaxed? How can you tell when a dog is feeling calm? Starting at the head, you look for a relaxed, open mouth, soft eyes, and normal breathing. When a dog is happy, his eyes appear bright, they make contact with you, they are engaging, and very little of the whites of the eyes are visible.

Photo credit: Jackie Lessing

When a dog is unruffled and stress-free, his ears will be in a more normal position. By definition, "normal" will depend on the breed of dog and the dog as an individual since each dog has a slightly different "relaxed" ear posture: some dogs' ears go straight up, some dogs' ears hang down, and some stick out at the sides. These differences in individual dogs are where learning to keenly observe your clients comes into play and will be of great help. At the other end of the dog, you're looking for a tail that is wagging, loose and wiggly, and possibly thumping on the ground—a combination that's generally a sign of a happy dog!

Fear, Anxiety, and Stress

Now let's discuss what animals, and specifically dogs, look like when they are worried, anxious, or stressed.

Let's start with some body-language descriptions. Beginning with a dog's head, an anxious dog may have his ears pinned back, his mouth tight. His lips may be pursed as well and perhaps also raised to show the canines. There might also be barking, or other vocalizations, such as growling, which serves as a warning sign prior to escalation. When a dog is preparing to bite, his teeth may be bared with his mouth puckered in such a way that the teeth are visible.

A dog's brow might look furrowed. Anxious dogs might also

pant excessively. You may note what are known as avoidance behaviors. For example, the dog might turn away to avoid eye contact or you might see the whites of his eyes as he looks in another direction.

Photo credit: Anne Francis

When a dog is ready to fight or bite, his eyes may be fixed in a hard stare, or he might overtly look away. You might also observe the combination of both the body appearing stiff and the whites of his eyes showing at the same time.

A dog's ears may be pinned back or flat and close to his head and he may seem to be backing away or leaning in the opposite direction. This behavior would indicate a frightened dog that could potentially bite if provoked. A dog's mouth may suddenly shut and there may be rapid panting, lip licking, and/or drooling.

At the other end of the dog, you can watch for the dog's tail carriage as an indicator of anxiety or stress. For most dogs, the tail carriage is easy to see; however, for some animals with cropped tails, this may be more difficult to discern. Nevertheless, try to note where the tail is located as it can be a good indicator of a dog that is experiencing fear, anxiety, or stress. An anxious dog may have his tail between his hind legs. Or the tail may be standing up stiffly and erect in the air.

Photo credit: Jay Andors

All the above-mentioned signs are important indicators of a dog's overall mood. When a dog is ready to bite, any combination of these body language signals may be present. It's also important to look at the dog's overall body posture for signs of discomfort. Is the dog trembling? Is the dog pacing? Is the dog displaying a "frozen" body position? Or a "shake-off," as if the dog is shaking off water (when he isn't wet)? Also, as you approach the dog, he may exhibit an overall body avoidance behavior which might look like he is backing away, or trying to hide by crouching down or curling up. Dogs may also express nervousness and a lack of comfort by lying on their backs and exposing their bellies.

While avoidance behaviors are often very obvious, there are other less obvious behaviors that also indicate stress, known as displacement behaviors, Displacement behaviors are any behaviors that occur out of context, and are simply ways in which a dog may communicate that it would like to "change the subject" when feeling uncomfortable.

Examples of displacement behaviors include yawning when not tired, panting when there's no exertion, shaking off when completely dry, or licking lips when no food is present. Other displacement behaviors you may observe could be scratching, tongue-flicking, sneezing, yawning, blinking, turning away, or sniffing the ground. Indicators of this type of anxiety might also include urinating or defecating.

Photo credit: Anne Francis

Again, all the above signs, occurring individually or in combination, will often indicate the degree of stress that a dog is experiencing.

Once you are better able to recognize these signs, you can attempt to address the cause of the stress and treat it accordingly. As noted, there are varying degrees and many different manifestations of stress. Learning to become aware of a dog's stress signals can help greatly in preventing a dog's anxiety from escalating, can save you time in the long run, and certainly can help to avoid injuries to both you and the dog.

Sometimes stress is a good thing because it enables an animal to learn. Moderate stress builds resilience. Extreme stress, however, may make it very difficult to groom an animal as it increases the amount of cortisol, serotonin and other neurotransmitters that trigger the fight or flight mechanism. This difficulty can cause the animal to immediately learn that the grooming shop, grooming table, and groomer are things to avoid at all costs.

Thus, generally speaking, once you learn what anxiety looks like, you want to work toward avoiding situations that cause the dog's anxiety to escalate, as there might be dangerous results that could include your being bitten, and/or the dog's getting injured. The better you become at recognizing stress, the more you will be able to differentiate between quickly changing scenarios.

Sometimes a dog may bark or growl in a playful way. However, at other times he might bark or growl as a warning or threat. Signs of stress could occur as isolated events or in combination. Learning how each individual dog is feeling at a particular time throughout the grooming process--by understanding and recognizing the signs--will allow you to alter your grooming plan them before the situation deteriorates.

This will enable you to make the process safer and more comfortable for everyone.

TIP: *Taking some additional time to help all dogs--but especially a fearful dog--feel comfortable will go a long way toward building trust and confidence in you and your shop. If a fearful dog arrives at your venue, an example of a strategy that you can use to start off on the right paw is to play the "on and off" game.*

The fearful dog on the table: The "on and off" game

To begin, start by putting the dog on the table, treating, and then taking the dog off the table. If at all possible, allow the dog to get on and off the table unassisted. Repeat this series a few times in a row, and then allow the dog to take a break and walk around the room a bit.

Keep repeating this process, gradually extending the time that the dog stays on the table. The individual temperament of the dog will determine how long you are able to play this game. You will want to stop before the dog becomes anxious, so try to go through the series (on/off) a few times in a row, and finish on a positive note.

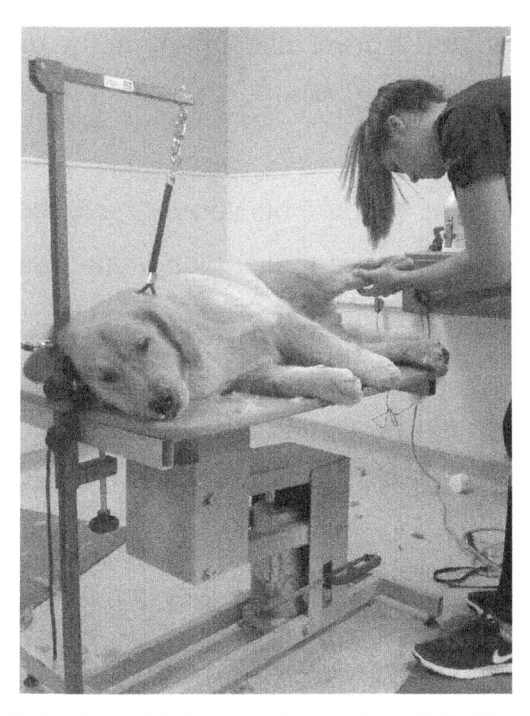

Photo credit: Kimberly Malinski & Casey Ann @ PetSpas & Suites, Colonie, NY

Stationing comfortably on the grooming table is a critical skill for any dog, especially a frightened one. This is where observation skills come in very handy. You can use the photos in this book as a reference point for stress vs. relaxed body language to help you gain fluency in determining how the dog is responding.

Remember, it is always better to stop before pushing the dog over his threshold. If need be, consider doing this exercise in two, separate, short sessions, and charge a nominal fee for these appointments. This is a good long-term investment for the dog's family, and a great investment for the groomer in terms of gaining a lifelong client.

Continue to play the "game" until you perceive that the dog is beginning to like it. Be sure to pair high-value treats with this activity throughout the game.

Once things are going well, consider finishing up the game—you always want to quit while you're ahead!

When the dog will stand comfortably on the table without trying to move away or get off the table, it's time to start to reinforce standing still. Should you find that you need additional assistance with this (or any other part of the exercises), you can always set up a private session via Skype or Zoom with Jay Andors who specializes in husbandry. Fellow co-author/trainer, Terrie Hayward, would also be a great resource as well!

3 CONCEPTS OF DESENSITIZATION AND COUNTER-CONDITIONING

Counter-conditioning and desensitization are two techniques often used in conjunction with each other in order to help dogs feel less fearful and more comfortable with places, people, objects, and environments. Basically, moving at a pace the dog feels comfortable with, and pairing an experience with something that the dog enjoys, are the key points of these science-based methods. Some of the most skilled and highly regarded individuals in the field of animal behavior further define these terms for us as follows.

According to Jean Donaldson in her book, *Mine* (2002),
> Systematic desensitization is a technique that was originally developed by behavioral psychologists to treat people with anxiety and phobias. The subject was exposed to a fear-invoking object or situation at an intensity that does not produce a response. If you are terrified of ants, for example, your first hierarchy rung might involve showing you a cartoon of a pink, unrealistic ant. If necessary, you would first view it at a distance. The idea is that you wouldn't be the slightest bit afraid (hopefully). The intensity, in this case, degree of realism and proximity, is very gradually increased and is contingent upon the

subject continuing to feel okay. A hierarchy is developed at the beginning of the treatment, ranging from the easiest to most difficult level versions of the stimulus.

Karen Pryor Academy defines counter-conditioning as:
Pairing one stimulus that evokes one response with another that evokes an opposite response, so that the first stimulus comes to evoke the second response. For example, a dog is afraid of men wearing hats. When a man wearing a hat approaches, the dog is repeatedly fed his favorite food. The goal is to replace the animal's apprehension with the pleasure elicited by the food. Counter-conditioning must be done gradually, however; if the process is rushed, the favorite food may take on the fear association instead (clickertraining.com/glossary/17).

These two concepts are key in helping a dog to feel safe, comfortable, and/or to change his previously negative associations with tools, situations, or people, to a conditioned emotional response (CER) that is pleasant and relaxing.

Meet and Treat

In order to help a dog feel comfortable in the grooming shop, we need to start at the beginning. This includes his very first interaction with the shop and groomer. We start by teaching the dog that the groomer and/or the groomer's shop are not scary. We begin by reinforcing calm behavior, and we do this by inviting prospective clients, especially those with new puppies, to come with their dogs for a visit.

This visit may be called the "Meet and Treat," which is a term coined by Jay Andors, co-author. The goal of this is to look for opportunities to use treats to reinforce any calm behavior. In this way we help the dog to build up a positive and pleasant association with the groomer and the shop.

Let's break down the concept of reinforcing behavior. Science tells us that behaviors that are positively reinforced will be repeated. We also know that more effective behavioral changes come by simply ignoring what we don't like—which only means not providing attention for the unwanted behavior--but at the same time reinforcing the behaviors that we like and want to see repeated.

According to an article (Michaels, n.d.) on the website of

Victoria Stilwell (television celebrity, positive reinforcement trainer, and behavior consultant): "As it turns out, it's scientifically sound advice to be nice to your dog." This is great news!

An example of what we are referring to can be found in this scenario: When a dog is sitting patiently on the table prior to having his nails clipped, that nice sitting behavior should be reinforced. Instead of waiting until the dog moves and won't hold his paw still for grooming, you want to be proactive and reinforce that second or two of nice, calm sitting and waiting. Be sure not to miss those small opportunities that allow you to recognize and reinforce behavior that you like!—and, rather than becoming angry/providing attention when the dog won't hold his paw still for trimming, be certain to recognize those quiet, still, moments of calm.

Basically, more often than not, we allow desired behaviors to just pass by without a thought, but when a behavior that we don't like occurs—for example, the dog begins to bark at someone—we scold the animal or react in some punitive way. Instead of responding to the behavior that we don't like, try looking specifically for something the dog is doing that you do like—in this case, "not barking," i.e., the silent moments between barks—and make a point of reinforcing those moments (however brief) with a pat or treat while ignoring the unwanted (barking) behavior. If the dog still seems to be displaying excitable or anxious behavior, this would be a good time to take a short break and allow the dog to relax off the table.

Even more to the point, we may have the dog at the grooming shop for several hours without realizing that he has been exhibiting behaviors that we like the whole time—such as, lying down quietly on the table, or just waiting and hanging out nicely, or perhaps coming over to you voluntarily. These are three great examples of things that dogs do in shops every day which are, opportunities to reinforce great behaviors. A small, yummy treat, happy praise, or scratches under the chin, are examples of things that dogs often find reinforcing. Remember, reinforcing behaviors that we like means that we will see more of them!

Reinforcers

What exactly is a reinforcer? Imagine that reinforcers have a range on a scale from one to ten with ten being the top. Things that dogs may consider level "ten" reinforcers could be treats like chicken, freeze-dried lamb lung, dehydrated steak, or baked and dried hot dog bits. Level "eight" type treats are usually something like a commercial treat such as Zukes Mini's or Pet Botanics, with regular kibble often falling more around a level "one" on the dog's scale. Reinforcers can also be praise, play, toys, games, or choice (such as the opportunity to move away or take a brief break).

Who decides what is reinforcing? The individual dog will be the one to determine the level of the reinforcer. For example, I may ask a person to move and sit in a chair and in turn reinforce his behavior with a $100 bill; similarly, a dog might be willing to perform the same behavior for a hamburger. As such, we want to be sure that the reinforcer that we are offering is something that the dog finds valuable.

Catching the animal in the act of doing something that you like, and reinforcing that behavior, encourages him to try this behavior again. Each time you reinforce a behavior, you are actually reinforcing future behavior, as learning is a result of reinforced repetition! Keep reinforcing behaviors that you want to see repeated, and you'll have a happier, more relaxed grooming shop.

Markers

At points in this book we may also reference a marker. A marker is a signal that lets the dog know that the behavior he has just performed has earned him access to something that he finds reinforcing. Markers allow us to "pinpoint" the exact behavior that we like. In order for a marker to maintain its value, it needs to be paired with a reinforcer—normally a small food item. A marker can be a word, such as "yes" or "good"; a clicker (a small, plastic device that makes a "click" sound); a whistle, or even a visual or tactile gesture. While you can use your reinforcer without a marker, a marker adds precision to the communication exchange

Counter-Conditioning, Desensitization, and the Grooming Process

As noted, desensitization and counter-conditioning are two tools that can help an animal feel more comfortable. Therefore, you will want to skillfully use them in your daily interactions with dogs!

Photo credit: Jay Andors

As a reminder, desensitization is the process of working slowly, at the dog's pace, to gradually expose the animal, over time and at a distance, to something he doesn't initially feel comfortable around. An example would be with nail clippers.

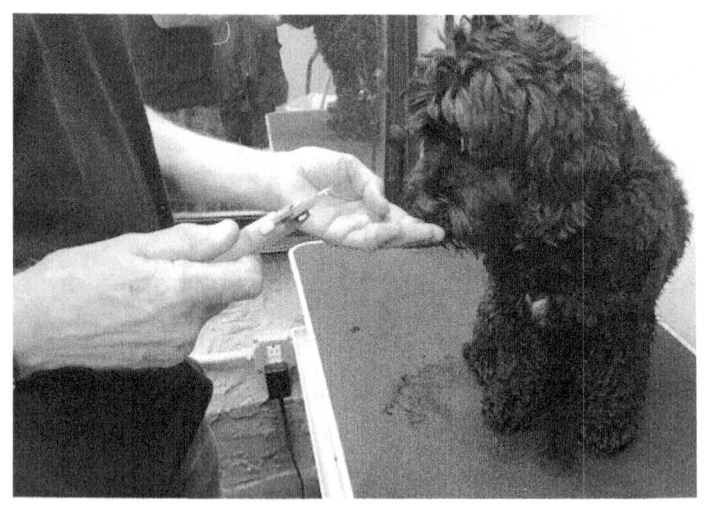

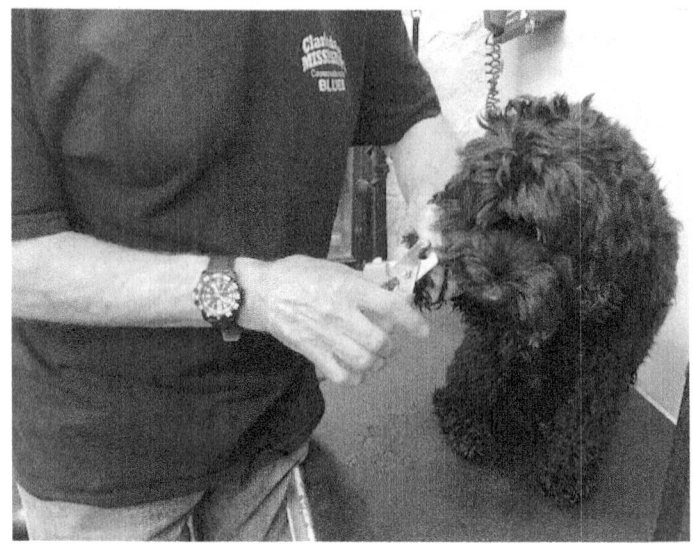

Photo credit: Jay Andors

Using desensitization, we would slowly, over a period of time, and at a pace that the dog indicates he's comfortable with via his body language, have the clippers move closer and closer to the dog. This process could even begin at home. Counter-conditioning involves pairing a "scary trigger" with something that the learner finds pleasant. In the nail clipper scenario, each time the dog initially chooses to look at the clippers, we offer a yummy treat. That is we want the appearance of the clippers to equal yummy treat. The order of operations is important here, as you want to be certain that clippers predict the treat and not the other way around. Often, as noted, desensitization and counter-conditioning are combined for the fastest results.

Another example of how desensitization and counter-conditioning would work in your shop might be with scissors. Many dogs might have a scary association with scissors, but by using desensitization and counter-conditioning we can help the dog to feel more comfortable with them. If the dog initially shows signs of stress in the presence of scissors, you might put them down on the table and wait for the dog to look at them calmly. When the dog does this, you can give him a yummy treat.

Another example might be with the electric clippers. If the dog shows signs of stress at the sound of the clippers, you may just turn them on and off several feet away from the dog to start, and treat for a calm response. This process then helps to create a positive conditioned emotional response (CER) whereby the sound of the clippers starts to mean that good things are going to happen! Here too, the order is key. Clicker noise predicts treat, not treat predicts scary clicker noise.

The same technique can be used to counter-condition (CC) to any tool. Let's give one more example, this time using a brush. We want "brush" to equal "happy, fun experience," so we will pair the brush with something that the dog really enjoys. We'll start slowly (using desensitization), perhaps by just showing the pup the brush and feeding a tiny bite of something considered (again, by the dog) to be delicious.

Next, we'll let the dog eat a piece of the deliciousness while we gently put the brush close to the dog's coat. Be sure that the brush appears before the treat. The following step would be to continue to work brushing longer and all around the dog's body while pairing the happy feeling from the treat with the brush. This process may be slow and will certainly require repetition—the question of how much and how long will depend on the dog's history, severity of anxiety, and the time that the caregiver and/or groomer is able to dedicate to the protocol of desensitization and counter-conditioning. However, keep in mind that if you rush through the process at the start, you may get the brushing done, but the process will prove to be exponentially more difficult the next time you bring out the brush. As such, dedicating additional time at the beginning—to help the dog feel relaxed around the brush via counter-conditioning and desensitization—will go a long way toward a dog that can calmly and easily tolerate brushing in the future.

If, for example, a dog has more severe anxiety about a certain grooming tool, you'll want to move even more slowly. In this case, with distance as your friend, you'll want to have the dog just look at the tool from far away at first. Then you can employ counter-conditioning too, whereby you feed the dog small pieces of something amazing while the tool is present, but nowhere near the dog. In this exercise, the "trigger" should be far enough away to not elicit fear, but close enough to be noticed. Very slowly you'll bring the tool closer to the dog. If you repeat this procedure enough times, eventually the tool will equate to happy feelings. Always be sure that the dog sees the potentially "scary" tool *before* you provide the treat. You want to be certain to do this in the correct order such that the tool equals the yummy treat vs. the yummy treat predicting the "scary" tool. This is a key component.

This process can be replicated with any specific tools that a dog is afraid of. It can also be used if a dog is anxious around all tools, and/or has never been in the presence of any. In such a case, you might need to perform this process with each individual tool. This activity can also be started in the home. Offering the service of teaching families how to collaborate with the processes of desensitization and counter-conditioning presents another opportunity for groomers to earn extra income. Again, the benefit here is that you will have a more relaxed dog that enjoys coming to the shop because he isn't frightened of the tools. This work also helps build a relationship with the dog's family, as they will feel like partners in the task of helping their dog to feel more relaxed and to enjoy the grooming experience.

While teaching these techniques to the dog's guardians, you might note that the family could also benefit from a correct-brushing lesson. You can explain to the owners that such a lesson will not only build the dog's confidence and keep his coat shiny but will also help to desensitize him to being brushed and handled at home and at the shop. This would then present the groomer with another opportunity to teach a skill that could net additional income.

TIP: *What should you do if you have a dog that is afraid to enter the shop? You can use desensitization and counter-conditioning to help him to feel more comfortable. For example, if a dog comes to the shop door and looks at you, we suggest tossing a treat on the* *ground. If the dog eats the treat, then looks up, we recommend tossing another treat. Now, if the dog is reluctant to go inside the grooming shop, you might take a walk with the guardian and dog, away from the shop, in order to desensitize the dog to your presence before going inside. This will also enable you to note the threshold (the point where the stress starts to be visible when the dog is approaching the shop), and to start to work on the Meet and Treat there, during which you can do a little training with the dog, reinforcing any calm behavior. You might ask for some easy behaviors such as a name recall, eye contact, sit, or any other behavior that the dog may know.*

The goal is to keep the dog engaged and to reinforce behaviors that you like. In this way you are building confidence, working on your relationship with the dog, and creating a positive conditioned emotional response (CER). We also find that this small engagement with the dog really impresses the owner, demonstrates compassionate care, and allows you some time to further expand upon and explain your services while you are meeting and treating.

Muzzle Comfort

Helping a dog feel comfortable while wearing a muzzle is a good example of how counter-conditioning and desensitization work. A sample training plan is noted below.

Sometimes it may benefit the groomer/handler and dog for the dog to wear a muzzle. As discussed earlier, rather than resorting to a "flooding" scenario and forcing the dog through a scary procedure with no hope of escape, and likely causing long-term negative associations and implications, a better route would be to take the time to desensitize and counter condition to muzzle-wearing. This can be worked on collaboratively, with clients following up at home.

Before beginning, be sure the dog is relaxed and comfortable. Have plenty of tiny (smaller than a dime), high-value, soft and tasty treats handy (think little pieces of chicken, hot dog, or cheese). A basket-type (Baskerville) muzzle is suggested as it allows the dog to eat, drink, and pant/breathe normally while wearing it. Be sure to use the correct size for your pup.

Sample training plan: Muzzle Desensitization

1. Hold the muzzle in your hand, but away from the dog. Click (or use another marker if possible) and treat for the dog being near it, looking at it, sniffing it, or showing any interest in the muzzle at all.
2. If the dog has previously had a bad/scary experience with a muzzle, he may not be able to remain relaxed when the muzzle is close by. In this case, an interim step would be to start by continuing to move the muzzle further and further away until the dog is calm, and that will be your beginning spot. Once the dog is calm, you slowly move the muzzle closer (maybe six inches at a time), until you

are again holding it in your hand. Then stop, and click and treat for the dog remaining calm.
3. Once the dog is able to remain relaxed, and shows calm interest in the muzzle, try holding it in your hand in such a way that you can put a treat in your palm and the dog needs to insert his nose into the muzzle to get it.
4. Allow the dog to voluntarily put his nose into the muzzle to retrieve the treat several times. Consider stopping the "game" here, and starting it up again at a new session. Keep in mind the idea, "Quit while you're ahead!"
5. Next, holding the muzzle in your hand, click and treat for the dog putting its nose into the muzzle (at this point you can still have a tiny treat inside the palm of your other hand for the dog to reach in and get).
6. With the dog's nose in the muzzle, the next step is to calmly bring the straps around behind his head. If the dog does not panic, mark (clicker or your verbal marker) and then treat.
7. Continue working slowly toward actually buckling the muzzle in place, and then click and treat for the dog calmly tolerating the muzzle on his face (not pawing or panting, etc.).
8. Repeat this several times, alternating between longer and shorter durations of muzzle-wearing (building up slowly with increments of only seconds of time at first).
9. Finally, generalize this behavior of muzzle-wearing to a

variety of locations that are pleasant for the dog (such as the park, a calm street in nice weather, encounters with warm and friendly people, etc.). In this way, the dog learns that wearing the muzzle anywhere, not just in one specific spot, will have a positive association (which would include being at the groomer's). While working on this step, continue to offer the dog treats through the muzzle for relaxed behavior.

If at any time the dog begins to show signs of anxiety and stress, back up to an "easier" step. You may also need to stop and repeat this process by breaking it up into multiple sessions. By going slowly, and at a pace that the dog can handle, you can succeed in transforming the muzzle from a scary tool, into one that predicts good things. In this way, you can help the dog feel comfortable with the muzzle, which, going forward, means a faster, easier, and safer process for all!

4 FIRST IMPRESSIONS

You may have heard the phrase, "You only have one chance to make a first impression." There is certainly truth to this saying. Before you even meet your new dog client, you might have spoken to the dog's family on the phone. Or the guardians may have come into your shop to inquire as to prices, schedules, and available services, etc. Creating a positive first impression with both people and dogs is a priority.

Meet and Treat interactions should be the first "in-person" greeting between you and the dog. This can be for new puppies as well as slightly older or adult dogs coming to the shop for the first time. Suggesting a Meet and Treat before the actual grooming takes place provides a good opportunity to learn more about the animal that you are going to be grooming and to work on relationship-building (with both dog and family). Making guardians feel comfortable is a key component to the interaction.

To get started, step one is to ask the family to stop by with their dog for the Meet and Treat. Remember, you'll move at a pace that the dog is comfortable with as relates to his proximity to you, the shop, and the tools. If things are going well, and the dog is relaxed during this initial interaction, you can also examine the dog's coat to see what needs to be done. Your use of a slow-paced greeting paired with treats should equate to a positive experience for the dog and his family.

Sometimes the dog and/or his guardian might already have a negative association with a groomer or a salon from a prior grooming experience elsewhere. In these instances, you want to pair the groomer and salon setting with something that the dog and his family have a good positive feeling about. This allows you to change the dog's response from, "eek=groomer" to "yay=groomer!" By arranging to meet with the dog and dog's family outside, treats in hand, you can begin this process even before the first grooming appointment is set up.

If the dog has severe anxiety related to simply arriving at the grooming location, the family may need to begin this process in the car outside, or even before getting close to the shop. You can help here by instructing families on how to slowly and positively allow the process of desensitization and counter-conditioning to help their dogs feel more comfortable.

As above, if the dog is afraid, due to previous fearfulness, of the groomers themselves, the same procedure of desensitization can be implemented. In other words, "see groomer from a distance"="feed amazing tiny bits of goodness." This, over time, will change the response from "groomer=scary" to "groomer=great!"

With the processes of counter-conditioning and desensitization (CC/DS), the dog does not have to perform any behavior in order to get the treat. The process only involves pairing the very positive stimulus (the yummy food) with the scary tool/person/situation.

While working on the above counter-conditioning and desensitization techniques, you will want to keep the three "D's" of training and behavior modification in mind. These include the following concepts: Distance, Duration, and Distraction. Each component should be increased slowly, at a rate that the dog is comfortable with. The dog's body language will denote his comfort level.

Again, beginning at a distance from the trigger will help the dog to feel less fearful initially. Starting with the trigger (groomer/brush/salon) in the distance while desensitizing will enable the sensation of trigger=good experience to begin to occur.

Small steps and mini-sessions, so as not to overwhelm the dog, are key factors in a desensitization plan. Be sure to introduce the "scary trigger" in tiny increments. You want the dog to note, "Trigger is present, and counter-conditioning with yummy items is occurring." Perhaps just one repetition may be enough to start with; possibly with another dog, multiple repeats may need to happen before stopping for a break.

While gradually building the dog's comfort level, distractions in the form of other dogs, a busy/noisy locale, or loud dryers and/or music may all contribute to the final environment that you'll work up to. Try to start with the least distracting situation possible and, as mentioned above, introduce things slowly and build in tiny increments.

Using the crucial components of desensitization and counter-conditioning via the science of behavior helps make permanent, lasting changes. These methods can enable you to change a dog's fearful response into one that is calm, and that is comfortable with you, the grooming tools and sounds, and your salon. With patience and consistency, groomers can help dogs and people to feel more relaxed about the process and, as such, build positive, long-term client relationships.

You decide: Choice as a Reinforcer

The next part of the interaction that you want to focus on is to recognize what a powerful tool "choice" is. Personal choice is considered a primary reinforcer. Most primary reinforcers are biological, such as food, water, or the ability to make decisions. A primary reinforcer means that we do not need to explain or condition something in order to understand that it is a good thing. In other words, the freedom to choose is a naturally occurring primary reinforcer. It also means that individual choice does not need to be paired with something else in order for it to have value.

If you do need to pair something, or "condition" it in order to have value, then it is called a secondary reinforcer. An example is currency. Money is not inherently valuable; however, when you pair it with things that you like, it then has worth. Thus, money is an example of a secondary reinforcer.

The most powerful type of reinforcers are primary reinforcers. As such, by using choice in our interactions with dogs that may be fearful about the grooming process, we are able to approach the experience in a positive way. Some examples of easy opportunities for the dog to insert choices into his time at the groomer's are as follows:

- The groomer crouching down, thereby allowing the dog to advance towards him (vs. the other way around);
- The groomer standing sideways and averting her eyes so as to not be looking straight at the dog, which may make her appear more approachable.

By allowing the dog to come to you, you are letting the dog choose where to move in the environment. Ultimately, the desired result is the same: you are near the dog. Moreover, by allowing the dog to *choose* to come to you, you have enabled a primary reinforcer to make the experience more pleasant.

Another example could be using choice with touch. By using a very light touch at the start, you can determine if the dog is comfortable with this interaction. His body language will express the level of comfort and, if this light touch is tolerated positively, you can take it as agreement that the dog might feel okay about being touched with a bit more pressure or duration. If, on the other hand, the dog moves his paw away, you can respect this choice, wait a moment, and then try again more slowly and/or more lightly. This approach recognizes and allows for the dog having some input in the process via choices.

Another instance where this might prove beneficial is when using restraint. Beginning with minimal restraint, wherever possible, allows the dog to feel more in control of the situation. Allowing choice in body position, as opposed to manually manipulating the dog into place, is another example of using choice as a primary reinforcer.

The final part deals with exposure. Allowing the dog to experience an exposure to a situation briefly at the start, and then building gradually to longer durations, as is demonstrated comfortable for the dog (via his body language), will help to improve the dog's overall experience. Respecting when the dog expresses that he is uncomfortable allows him to have a "say" in the interaction, and this choice can go a long way toward helping the dog better tolerate and ultimately find the experience less stressful.

The opposite of this approach would be a term known as "flooding." Flooding is when the dog is confined, cannot escape, and must endure the experience. Flooding as a tactic will not help the dog to change his response to the situation to a more positive one. Moreover, it will most likely create more anxiety and trepidation with being groomed at this moment, as well as with grooming situations going forward. In other words, if we were to use flooding to "force" a frightened dog through the grooming experience, the next time would be proportionally worse.

According to Victoria Stilwell ("Flooding," n.d., para. 4):
> In the majority of cases flooding only makes a dog more anxious and forces the dog to adopt different coping mechanisms such as fighting, irrespective of how many dogs there are, or shutting down – where

the dog becomes almost numb to the environment and behaves in a way that is truly out of character - an instinct that keeps him safe and ensures survival. This shut down lasts as long as the dog is in the flooding environment, and once back in his comfort zone, the dog is free to be able to show his true feelings again.

Often, folks may presume that the best approach is to just charge ahead and get through the grooming and just get it over with. However, this tactic is an example of "flooding," which will more likely than not result in fear, apathy, aggression, and/or escape/avoidance behaviors the next time the dog returns to the groomer's.

As a human example of flooding, let's say that you do not like snakes. If you were forced into a room filled with snakes (think scene from *Indiana Jones*!), you would not eventually feel better about snakes. Instead, the next time you saw snakes you might even be more fearful.

Instead, you want to basically do the opposite of flooding. That is, you want to move slowly and in such a manner that once you notice that the dog is getting tense or agitated, you stop and allow the dog to settle back down. Moving forward in this way may initially necessitate additional time; however, instead of creating an adverse experience, you will be teaching the dog that he can feel comfortable in these surroundings. This approach helps us to have a client who can easily tolerate—if not enjoy—the grooming process, which will ultimately speed things up going forward.

The Meet and Treat at the groomer's shop, discussed earlier, is a good example of how to help a dog feel comfortable in a potentially scary setting. Even before arriving at the groomer's, you can explain to clients how to create a nice, pleasant ride in the car where the destination happens to be the groomer's, but nothing scary happens. As an example, perhaps for the first drive over, the family just stops the car briefly at the front of the shop, gives the dog some treats for calm behavior in the car, and then leaves. Then, the next time, they may go inside, just take a stroll around for the Meet and Treat, and leave.

By doing this, the dog learns that going in the car does not always equal some fright-provoking end. Too, the dog then doesn't begin his anxiety before even getting to the groomer's. Dogs that can and do view car rides as part of the fun are relaxed and happy—which is a much better way to precede walking through the shop's front door.

To re-cap, by adjusting initial interactions and setting up Meet and Treats, using choice as a primary reinforcer vs. immediate restraint, and working slowly and at the dog's pace instead of employing flooding techniques, we can help dogs to enjoy and appreciate the grooming experience—which, in turn, makes for less stressful, safer, and speedier handling for groomer and family too!

Sample training plan: Meet and Treat

1. Plan to meet the dog and owner a few blocks away from the shop, if possible. Ideally, it would be good to meet there with plenty of treats on hand to give to the dog for any display of calm behavior.
2. Walk towards the shop with the dog and guardian. Treat the dog for paying attention to you or for any calm behavior while watching for any of the signs of stress that we discussed earlier, such as lip licking, yawning, backing away, etc. If the dog begins to display stressful body language, you may need to just stop, or back up to an easier location for the dog (further away from the shop or groomer). Plan to meet the guardian once again on another day, and repeat this process until the dog is comfortable walking up to and inside the shop. Set these Meet and Treats up throughout your day (for several different dogs) at times convenient for the guardians to stop by, and so you can also have some mini-breaks in your daily routine.
3. Once the dog is happy to see you (as determined by

appropriate body-language interpretation), reliably focused on you, and will easily accompany you to the shop, stop in the doorway and have a "party" with some really special treats. At this point you might try to pet the dog and give the treat at the same time. Allow the dog to approach you (vs. your going to him) and encourage him to come even closer by angling your body sideways (vs. direct, straight-on body language and eye contact, which can be intimidating). Have high-value treats on hand. During this phase you can use the time to begin to evaluate and judge the type of haircut the dog needs and where problems may be on his body with matting, etc. This is also an ideal time for you to you discuss with the guardian what has been done in the past with other groomers.

4. Continue providing treats for calm behavior and gently walk with the dog into the grooming room. Meanwhile, assess for things that might frighten the dog, such as the presence of scissors, the hair dryer, brushes, combs, nail clippers, the grooming table, and the tub. Make some quick notes (mental, and later, written for the files) on what environmental tools may be scary to this particular dog. Perhaps he has had a difficult history with some tools or certain parts of the grooming process.

5. Gently put the dog up on the table while continuing to treat frequently. If the dog will allow (that is, if the dog can

tolerate this part at this time) and signs of stress are absent, palpate the dog and assess his coat/nails/etc. Continue to offer the dog treats throughout this part of the process. If the dog displays other signs of stress or stops taking the treats (which may be a sign of stress), back up to an easier step (dog back on the floor) and/or take a break, or finish for the day.

6. At this point, depending on how things are going, you might be able to begin a dialogue with the dog. We do this by showing the dog our tools and treating for remaining calm. Demonstrate the scissors, clipper blades, clipper, and brushes while treating for calm behavior. You can hold the implements at a bit of a distance (arm's length) away at first and eventually, gradually, work at holding them closer to the dog. These sessions should be short, i.e., no more than five to ten minutes long. At this point, end the session and return the dog to his family member. You want the scenario to look like this: Show scissors to the dog at arm's length and treat for calm behavior. Repeat. If the dog remains relaxed, bring the scissors a little closer. Getting the scissors from arm's length distance to a few inches away from the dog may need to be broken up into more than one session if the dog is stressed. You are not doing any actual cutting during this step.

It is important to keep in mind that, ultimately, the grooming process is a long-duration behavior chain. Thus, these preliminary steps will help to get the dog used to longer and longer stays at the shop. This first shop interaction is a great time for you to really observe and assess the dog's responses and to plan ahead to make subsequent visits successful.

Remember that you are building a new relationship. You can explain to the owner that on the dog's regular grooming days, in addition to the actual grooming, you may also have to counter a long reinforcement history of what might have been a highly uncomfortable and stressful prior grooming experience elsewhere (for both guardian and dog alike). You can build this into your cost or you can offer it free of charge.

Scheduling these Meet and Treats throughout your day will give you a break from the grooming table and allow for one-on-one time with the guardians to build personal relationships. These meetings also serve as opportunities to sell the different services your shop may offer, such as daycare, specialty foods and products, boarding, etc. Depending on the individual client, you can charge for a service and/or use it to promote your business as well as other services that you might have available.

This coaching session is a good chance to also discuss any

other challenges the guardian may be having with the dog. If you can encourage the owner to talk about these concerns, you may learn of other areas of behavior that you can be of help with. Remember that because past experience and the consequences thereof have affected the dog's daily life, he might have problems with being handled that may not be limited to grooming—in fact, such repercussions usually show up in other situations as well.

The next possible place to begin (perhaps on the same day, if the dog is relaxed) would be with some easy conditioning to paw handling.

Remember to start with the basics at your first visit (post Meet and Treat). Keep in mind on this first grooming appointment that you can skip certain steps in order to accomplish the haircut. For example, you don't have to clean between the paw pads and you don't have to clip the nails. Too, if stressful, you don't have to clean the ears on this first visit either. This gives you a chance to charge the owner for the time you spend during this first grooming, as well as for the follow-up appointment to finish the job while ensuring more successful, relaxed future visits with the dog.

5 THE GROOMING PROCESS

When thinking about the grooming process, we can look at it like a chain of events. This can also be referred to as a behavior chain. Clickertraining.com defines a behavior chain as "an event in which units of behavior occur in sequences and are linked together by learned cues." The grooming process is just this—a series of events linked by cues that the dog learns along the way. These cues may be either positive or not so positive from the dog's perspective. As groomers, you can help the dog to learn to like, if not love, this behavior chain that results in a more calm and safe scenario for dog, family, and groomer alike.

The chain looks something like this: *Greeting—→Bathing—→Drying—→Nails—→Ear Cleaning—→Cut.* There are many opportunities in this chain to improve the dog's perception of the process!

Greeting

As we've noted, we want to begin with the Meet and Treat as a brand-new first introduction. Ideally, with a new puppy, it will look something like this: The dog comes to the shop excited about meeting people and exploring the smells. This is a good thing! As we want to see more of this enthusiastic behavior, you'll reinforce it with plenty of praise and treats. You are specifically looking for calm, loose body language.

Remember you may need to repeat the Meet and Treat more than once, especially if the dog is older or has had an unpleasant experience with grooming in the past. Next, you'll allow for a bit of extra time here for what will be considered the dog's very first grooming experience. Remember, you'll make up for this initial added time down the road by ultimately having a calm and easy-to-work-with dog! When introducing dogs to the grooming area, let them sniff around a bit to see what's going on. You want to reinforce nice, composed behavior with praise and treats while keeping any eye out for any signs of stress. As a reminder: calm, relaxed behavior should present as a loose and wiggly body with normal respiration rate, while a dog's anxious behavior may be indicated by the dog stiffening, freezing, or backing away.

Things to keep in mind during these early interactions at the groomer's are how the temperature, lighting, or flooring might affect the dog's first impression of the shop. This entire first introductory process to the shop itself should take no more than fifteen or twenty minutes. If the dog is demonstrating relaxed body language (as covered in Chapter 2), the dog's family can leave and then come back at the end of this vey short visit. Remember, the underlying goal of this introductory experience is to make it a positive one, which can be achieved by using your observational skills and adjusting your interactions to make sure the dog is as comfortable as possible.

After the visit, we suggest that you write down what you noticed going on with the dog together with any questions or recommendations you might have. For example, does the dog need to come again for another Meet and Treat?—or, do you think you can take it a step further at the next grooming visit? Was the dog comfortable with the sights and smells in the shop? Was there any time when the dog seemed to become more anxious? Which treats was the dog most responsive to? Making careful behavioral notes in the dog's chart is an important component to being sure to reliably and consistently address concerns. Remember to note observable and quantifiable behavior as opposed to using labels—which can "stick" and predispose people to negative connotations about the dog. Instead, jot down information about how the dog reacted and include body language communication.

TIP: *Observing dogs carefully during grooming sessions, and keeping good notes, is an important part of bringing about individual positive changes to the process for each dog. While many shops do this, you want to be sure that your notes are clear and detailed. Think about including observable behavior (like "ears relaxed" or* *"loose, wiggly body") vs. labels (such as "aggressive" or "stubborn"). These notes will help you to be better prepared for the next visit, too!*

If moving ahead at the next visit, again begin with a meeting where you treat and reinforce calm behavior. Allow the dog to sniff around once more, and reinforce calm behavior with happy praise and yummy treats. This time, you might take the dog into the grooming area of the shop and allow him to run around a bit. You might then want to put some tasty treats or perhaps the dog's breakfast (you can suggest that the owner bring it along) on the table. You can let the dog eat his breakfast there while you lay out, on the same table, the different tools you will be using. As the dog notices the tools, encourage him with some nice words of praise, and then give him a special treat for noticing the tools and remaining calm. In other words, if the dog sees that you have placed the scissors or the clippers on the table, but remains relaxed and continues to eat, you will want to reinforce this behavior.

Bathing and Drying

If all is still going well, you might then want to put the puppy in the tub, with no water, and let him sniff around. Maybe put some tiny high-value treats in the tub. Then remove the treats and turn the water on for a few seconds while feeding him the treats. Note the dog's reaction.... is he startled by the sound? If he just noticed the water running, but without any anxious reaction, give him some more of the same treats. On the other hand, if the puppy is really startled by the sound, then back up the process to the step where he can remain calmly on the table, and continue to reinforce relaxed behavior there.

Photo credit: Anne Francis

A good marketing strategy can result from the above approach of using the slow and careful process of desensitization and counter-conditioning to create a positive association with bath time. You can offer this "First Time Dog/Puppy Grooming Intro" free of charge or at a nominal fee, interspersing these new grooming clients throughout your grooming day schedule.

Ultimately, you want dogs to believe that going to a grooming salon is a pampering, luxurious experience that is relaxingly pleasant and not terrifying at all.

Photo credit: Tamson Leanne with Otter

The basics of bathing and drying consist of a series of steps before the bath. These include actions such as cleaning the ears, clipping the nails, hygienic shaving around the rectum and genital area at the lower belly, cleaning in-between the paw pads, and brushing the teeth (clickertraining.com/node/4743). Each of these procedures is uncomfortable at best, and can be terrifying and painful at the other end of the spectrum. Following this series of steps, traditional instruction would then suggest the bath. You'd think that this could be an enjoyable and relaxing process for the dog—and in some cases it is. However, in the case of a dog that has had a terrifying reinforcement history in the grooming process, the bath is just another step on the ladder of reactivity.

After the bath comes the dryer. While some dogs love this part of the day, a dog that is terrified of the grooming process might already be at the top rung of the proverbial stress ladder, with his body full of cortisol and serotonin and other neurotransmitters. This would be a situation in which the dog is now so uncomfortable that it would be incredibly difficult for him to become calm and remain still for what should be the easiest part of the grooming process; the haircut.

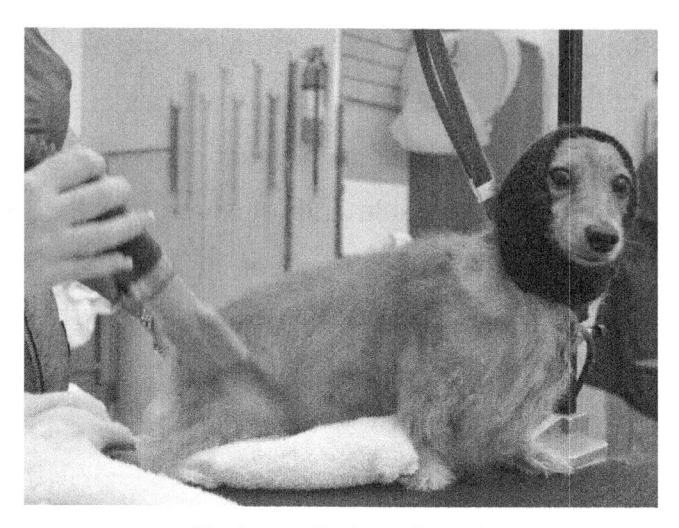

Photo credit: Anne Francis

What we recommend here is a variety of "tweaks" to this schedule that will allow you to manipulate and adapt the process to each individual dog client that comes into your shop so that the experience can be as pleasant as possible. This will ultimately result in an easier and quicker groom for the dog, and a safer and less stressful process for the groomer.

Families can do a lot at home to help get a "jump start" on behaviors with things that you want them to feel more relaxed about in the grooming shop. Another one of these behaviors that can be practiced at home is bathing.

Sample training plan: Bathing at Home

We can greatly increase a dog's comfort level with bathing by encouraging families to help out at home with the training. As such, we suggest that you provide the following guidelines to the guardian re working daily on a bath with a new puppy. This plan lays out specific steps that, over time, will lead to a dog's becoming much more relaxed with the bathing process. This procedure can help create a positive emotional response that associates good things happening in the tub (meals and treats) with the experience of being in the tub and bathing.

1. Put a towel or rubber mat inside the tub and start to feed the dog his meals right there in the tub. For a puppy, a towel may suffice; however, a rubber mat really provides a solid footing. An issue with porcelain tubs is that they can be very slippery.
2. At various times throughout the day, gently put the puppy in the tub and just give him some high-value treats there. This will help to prepare your puppy in two ways. First, visually: The tub becomes a cue that good things occur there (food and treats). Next, emotionally: By the family's building this positive association at home with the tub, the puppy should already have a good feeling about it when he arrives at the groomer's for his first bath.

A preliminary bathing process at home can result in an adult dog feeling more comfortable in the tub as well. And, whether or not the dog is frightened of being bathed (not uncommon), it is never too late to employ desensitization and counter-conditioning to help him feel more relaxed about this part of the grooming routine. In either case, you would proceed as follows:

1. Begin by starting to feed the dog near the tub.
2. Next give the dog a treat just for looking at the tub.
3. Then, give the dog a treat just for looking at the tub, but now place the treat on the ledge of the tub so that the dog has to get closer to the tub to retrieve it. In this way, we are reinforcing the dog's voluntarily moving closer to the tub and associating good things (the treat) with the tub. Make sure the mat is positioned safely inside the tub so that the dog is not in danger of slipping.
4. Repeat this process many times until the dog is actively looking for the treat on the ledge.
5. Next, when the dog looks for the treat on the ledge of the tub, click (or use another marker if you like) and provide another treat inside the tub for the dog to retrieve.
6. Gradually, over time, you will change the placement of the treat so that you position it inside the tub with the ultimate goal of getting the dog to jump into the tub (provided that he can safely do this).
7. Once the dog jumps into the tub, and you have clicked and placed another treat in the tub, you can then click for his being inside the tub, and place the next treat back on

the outside of the tub. The goal here is to get the dog used to going in and out of the tub by himself.

Once the caregiver has practiced the above at home, the plan below can take place at the groomer's shop.

Groomers and bathers can ask families if they have done the recommended preceding practice at home. Once that has been confirmed, it would be a good idea to repeat steps a few times at the groomer's just to generalize the dog's comfort level to the shop tub. This means that you'll want to back up to a couple of the easier steps to "warm up" the process for the dog.

If the shop tub doesn't have steps or is raised up off of the ground, an interim step might include shaping the dog to comfortably allow being picked up and placed in the tub. Be sure to pair treats with the experience to create a positive association.

Once the dog will go in the tub expecting treats, you are ready to start to turn on the water. This might require you to repeat the picking-up process several times in order for the dog to feel comfortable. It may also be advantageous to break this step up into several sessions where you repeat this piece as well.

Sample training plan: Bathing at the Groomer's

1. With the pup now in the tub, turn the water on and off. Treat for the dog remaining calm as you turn the water on and off. Continue turning the water on and off, and keep treating for calm, relaxed behavior. The goal is to get a high rate of reinforcement going, as we really want to create a great emotional response to being in the tub.
2. Once the dog is comfortable with the water being turned on and off, the groomer or bather can start to wet the dog. This part of the process should proceed slowly, and care should be taken not to startle the dog.
3. Now that the dog is wet, if not using a bathing system, put some of your shampoo mixture on the dog. A recommendation is to mix the shampoo with water in a bottle or container prior to bathing. This way, the shampoo will immediately rinse off the animal because it is in solution, which makes this part of the process much easier.
4. Prior to putting shampoo on the dog, it is recommended that you use SafeEye drops. These drops are a mineral oil ophthalmic that protects the eyes from the burning sensation of shampoo, which can be very irritating.
5. Next, apply the shampoo and work it into the dog's coat. If the dog seems stressed, you might be rubbing too hard. Keep in mind that dogs are very sensitive to this as there

are many neurotransmitters located in the hair follicles.

As a final note on bathing, the Meet and Treat may be a good time to assess the dog's reaction to being in the tub (without water) and/or to also being picked up. Depending upon the dog's level of comfort with this, you may or may not be able to proceed at this point with introducing the above tools and situations related to the bathing process.

Nails

Let's talk about nail clipping for a moment. How important is nail clipping? Should a dog that hates his nails being clipped or paws being touched have his nails clipped as the first procedure in the grooming behavior chain? Would this approach help to create a smooth flow of events? We think not. Instead, we recommend thinking about how to help the dog feel secure right from the start, and then, step-by-step, working to increase his confidence and comfort level before proceeding with the clipping. Using the concepts of desensitization and counter-conditioning will go a long way toward helping a dog to not feel fearful about the nail-clipping experience.

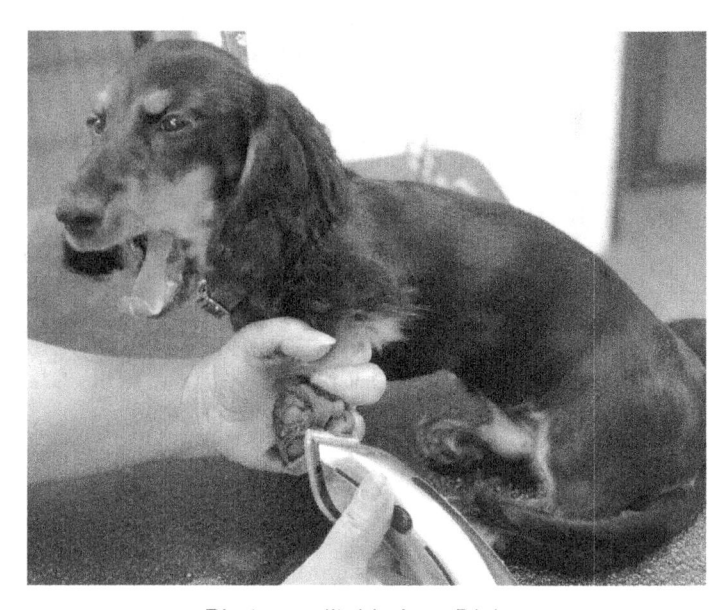

Photo credit: Lindsey Dicken

Once a dog is completely comfortable with his paws being handled, you can begin to combine two behaviors: relaxed paw-handling behavior with calm behavior in the presence of clippers or nail file. At this point, be sure to go slowly; taking an approach at a level that the dog feels comfortable with will ultimately pay helpful dividends. Once the dog is relaxed with the combination of these behaviors, nail clipping would be a next logical step.

A sample plan could be a one-hour lesson in which you might include a brush-out. While you are talking to the guardian and brushing out the dog, you can start to coach the owner in the steps needed to shape this cooperative nail behavior. The family's also working on this process at home can be a big help in terms of increasing the dog's comfort levels with paw handling in the grooming shop.

There are some aspects of the total behavior related to nail clipping that need to be trained separately before being put together. As such, we first need to help the dog feel comfortable with paw handling, and then, next, we help the dog feel comfortable in the presence of the nail clippers. Once these pieces are developed individually (paw handling and clipper proximity comfort), they can be put together. Note that this is another principle from Karen Pryor: "Train one criterion [or aspect] at a time" (see "The Modern Principles..." in Chapter 8). This doesn't mean that you can't eventually train for both aspects to occur together—in this case, the dog being calm in the presence of the clippers while allowing his paw to be held for longer and longer durations. It just means that you must first have a separate training session for each part.

Remember, if you can break down every aspect of what's required to where it's easily accepted by the dog, you will ultimately be more successful in ensuring a better relationship and more relaxed handling for future appointments.

We start with paw handling:
Sample training plan: Paw Handling
Begin with the dog in a relaxed position. This might be on the

floor or up on the table.

1. To start, gently touch the dog's paw. Then, if the dog does not pull his paw away or offer any other indicators that he is stressed, offer a treat.
2. Next, if Step 1 has gone well, consider gently holding the dog's paw, then treating for relaxed body language.
3. Once more, if the dog is still relaxed you can now move to holding his paw for a little bit more time (two seconds), then treating for continued relaxed behavior.
4. Continuing on, if the dog remains calm, you can hold the paw while applying a bit of pressure (squeeze gently), then treat for continued relaxed behavior.
5. Be sure to "bounce" between longer-holding and easier gentle-touching versions so that the dog does not decide that he doesn't like the "game," as it is getting harder with each step. Instead, make it fun by interspersing some easier steps so that the dog can get a comfortable "win" in.
6. Continue treating calm behavior for varied levels of touching, picking up, holding, squeezing, manipulating, and moving the paw around, always providing feedback (in the form of the click and treat) for calm behavior.

Tip: *If at any time the dog becomes uncomfortable, you will want to back up to an easier step or stop the session and re-visit the process at another time.*

Now that you've worked on paw handling, the second aspect, helping the dog feel comfortable in the presence of nail clippers, can be trained, after which the two behaviors can be put together.

Sample training plan: Clipper Proximity

1. Treat for any calm behavior around the nail clippers. Have the nail clippers present next to an empty food bowl (empty at this point); the dog will come to the bowl. Now that the dog is motivated to come to this area where the clippers are, we can help teach him to eat in the presence of the clippers.
2. Next, owners can help out at home by starting to introduce the clippers at other times throughout the day, but always pairing the appearance of the clippers with a delicious treat (see step four below).
3. Back at the shop, as the dog gets comfortable with having the clippers nearby in the environment, perhaps now try having the clippers in your hand with a bowl of treats that the dog really likes (high-value) handy. Reinforce any calm behavior, such as approaching you to access the treat. Use this time to observe the dog carefully. If the dog shies away, this means that he's not comfortable with the clippers. If this happens often, it might be a good idea to approach the same process with an emery board or nail

file in order to begin in a less threatening manner. Repeat these steps until the dog is really comfortable with these objects, increasing proximity to the paw little by little.
4. Ideally, these steps should be followed up at home. You can sell families their own nail clippers for at-home practice with their dogs. The more that you are able to encourage guardians to get involved with their dogs, the more confident they will be around the dogs, and the more their dogs' quality of life will improve, thereby providing more comfort and joy for the whole family unit.

As a side note regarding nail clippers, some dogs have strong emotional responses to just the sight of the clippers. This may be due to a previous experience. If you notice that a certain instrument causes the dog to become very fearful, you can do a number of things. One alternative, as mentioned above, is to perhaps temporarily use a regular nail file or emery board. There are also Dremel-style filing tools available. Even with an alternative tool it is important to desensitize and counter-condition to be sure to create a positive association for the dog!

If you see that the dog is frightened of nail clipping, this is a great time to offer your expertise in a private coaching session. You can use the time to teach the guardian(s) how to help shape the dog's behavior and responses so that the dog will be able to voluntarily cooperate in nail clipping and/or filing. It is more important to think about the long term here, especially if the nails are not that overgrown and nail trimming is not critical. If the dog is stressed, it would be better to avoid clipping for now and work on the dog's comfort level to help de-escalate the stress. This translates to easier, safer clipping for both dog and groomer at (all) future visits.

Tip: *You might want to think about developing a class where you can charge a fee and have five or six people at a time come to the shop after hours where you can teach how to do some "homework" around nail trims. This structured instruction will go a long way toward making the nail trim experience much more pleasant, safer, and ultimately quicker! At the class you can also promote other services and products. Grooming shops today are not only places where dogs just get haircuts. Shops are full-service facilities that often include boarding, daycare, training, and products for sale such as food, grooming tools, and clothing.*

Ear Cleaning

Dogs may sometimes also be averse to people touching or cleaning their ears. Remember, if the dog is uncomfortable, rather than forcing the issue, take the time now to address this with care so that you will ultimately save time in the long run. In terms of ear cleaning, many studies suggest that nature and natural selection have given dogs hair in their ears to protect the ear canal. In view of this, rather than arbitrarily pulling the hair out, you might just be able to clean it. You can use a liquid canine ear-cleaning product, which can be placed on a cotton ball to wipe out the ears.

Remember to stop and check on how the dog is doing. This is key, as moving forward with a procedure that may be uncomfortable, when a dog is anxious, can have long-lasting consequences. A one-time aversive learning event can set the tone for future visits. We want to be certain not to squander our only opportunity to make a positive first impression!

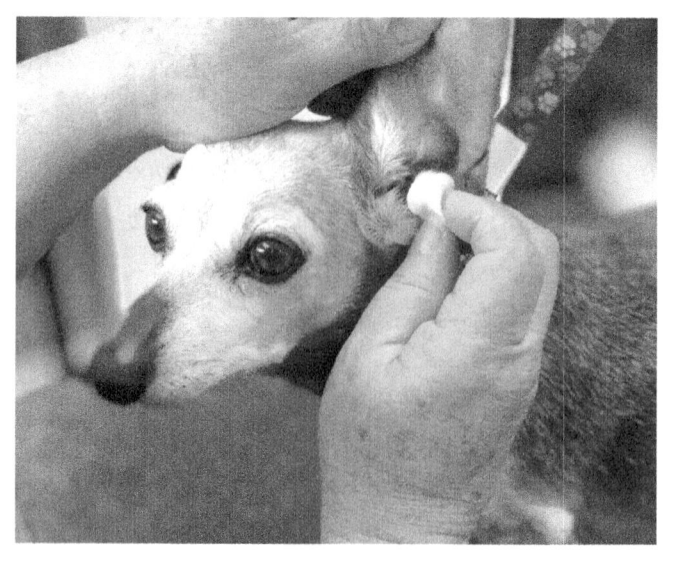

Photo credit: Lindsey Dicken

Following is a training plan that you can utilize as a guide in helping a dog feel more comfortable and relaxed while having his ears cleaned.

Sample training plan: Ear Cleaning
Before beginning, be sure that the dog is in a relaxed state. You'll need to have cotton balls and some high-value treats available. It is recommended that you work on stationing behavior (sample plan in Chapter 10) prior to the ear-cleaning plan.

1. First, touch the dog's ear gently for one second with just one finger. Click (keep clicker away from ear when clicking to avoid frightening the dog) or mark with your verbal marker and provide a small yummy treat.

Tip: *As a reminder you can always use a verbal marker instead of a clicker; if using a verbal marker, you can replace the "click" with the word "good" or "yes," but just as with the clicker, you will want to follow the marker with a treat!*

2. Then, touch the other ear gently for a second. Click or use your verbal marker "yes." Again, if using a clicker, keep the clicker away from the dog's ear.
3. Next, touch the ear gently for two seconds. Mark and treat for calm behavior.
4. Then, touch the ear for four seconds. Click or use your verbal marker "yes" and treat, provided that the dog remains relaxed. If the dog is anxious or reactive in any

way, back up to Step 1.

Tip: *You will notice that in order to build the duration of the animal's allowing you to manipulate his ear, you first have to build a positive reinforcement history of the animal allowing his ear to be touched. This is a very important point and one that is worth investing the time to train!*

5. Now you will start to bounce back and forth between a shorter and a longer touch. As such, this time touch the ear for only two seconds. Click or use your verbal marker "yes" and treat.
6. Then, touch the dog's ear for a second. Click or use your verbal marker "yes" and treat.
7. Now touch for five seconds. Click or use your verbal marker "yes," and treat again for relaxed behavior.
8. Touch for two seconds. Click and treat.
9. Touch for eight seconds. Click and treat.

Tip: *The total amount of time needed for an ear cleaning will be determined by the individual dog—however, a suggestion may be that you ultimately shape the dog to allow thirty seconds for a procedure that requires only holding the ear for ten seconds, so that when you actually do the procedure, it seems "easy."*

10. Once you have a long enough duration of only touching the dog's ears, it's time to add the second component.

The next phase will be to hold the dog's ear with one hand and touch the inside of the ear with a cotton ball or Q-tip. Repeat the steps above while adding in the new element of the behavior – the cotton ball – but reducing the touch time to a much shorter duration at first, as we have now added a new element.

11. Touch and hold the ear for two seconds. At the same time, use the other hand to touch the inside of the ear with a cotton ball for one second. Click and treat if the dog does not try to react, move away, etc.
12. Touch and hold the ear for one second (no cotton ball). Click and treat.
13. Touch and hold the ear for four seconds. During these four seconds, touch the ear with a cotton ball for a second. Click and treat. Little by little, you want to build up a longer and longer duration before adding in the next element—moving the cotton ball around.
14. Next, touch and hold the ear for four seconds while you gently move the cotton ball around inside the ear for a second. Click or use your verbal marker "yes," and treat for calm behavior.
15. Touch and hold the ear for two seconds while you gently move the cotton ball around the inside of the ear for a brief second or two. If the dog is calm, click and treat; if the dog reacts by showing stress or by trying to move away, back up a few steps and slowly try again. Make it

easy for the dog to get it "correct"!

16. Touch and hold the ear for six seconds while gently moving a cotton ball around inside the ear for two to three seconds. Be sure to click (or use your "yes" verbal marker) and treat for the dog remaining calm throughout the process.

You can encourage clients to set up training sessions at home where they begin to play this game with their dog. Even just pairing tasty treats with some gentle ear handling will help with the process.

You will notice that as the above steps advance, they do not get more difficult, but rather bounce between more challenging versions and easier ones. This prevents the dog from becoming more frustrated and fearful, and deciding that he doesn't like the "game."

6 CHALLENGES AND SCIENCE

The objection that groomers and caregivers may have to a more positive or gentle approach might be able to be summed up in one sentence: It takes more time, and may cost more in the long run. Most families just want to have their dogs come in and be beautifully groomed.

However, we suggest that not only do we perform a high caliber of grooming, but we also propose a different marketing strategy/plan with a positive note and a new message that will build better client return.

Simply put, all that we have to do is explain to caregivers, in a clear and concise manner, that the investment of some extra time and perhaps a slight additional cost at the beginning for shaping the grooming process, will pay huge dividends in the future, especially since grooming is a reoccurring event in the dog's life.

Scientifically, we know that stress produces cortisol, and that once it starts to surge through the animal's veins, it takes time to dissipate. This means that, for example, if the dog comes to the grooming shop and becomes extremely stressed out, the impact may be felt for some time afterward. This may translate into a dog that is more reactive to perceived "threats," and/or is more uncomfortable being handled and petted, even by his family members, until he returns to a calm or more homeostatic state.

Photo credit: Samantha Sheppard

Taking this approach that places great emphasis on the dog's physical and mental well-being can also translate to a great marketing strategy. Clients who frequently come into the shop present opportunities to sell more products. Additionally, such clients build relationships with you and your staff, which equates to the likelihood of their sharing this good experience with others.

7 COOPERATIVE CARE

Now that we have explained why we want to focus on helping dogs to cooperate in their own care—that it's safer, healthier, and, over the long term, garnishes more loyal and productive clients—just how do we go about doing this? How do we actually develop cooperative behaviors? Let's start at the beginning. Step one is to work towards creating a positive conditioned emotional response (CER) with the groomer, the tools, the sounds, the shop, and the overall experience.

As noted in the previous chapter, the grooming process is what we can consider to be a long-duration common behavior chain. "A behavior chain is an event in which units of behavior occur in sequences and are linked together by learned cues" (clickertraining.com/node/111).

Teaching your dog to cooperate comfortably with handling is very important. Cooperative handling can be taught by constantly desensitizing and counter-conditioning to new and potentially scary tools, people, and situations. Desensitization is defined as repeatedly exposing the dog, in tiny doses, over time, to the object or procedure in question. This happens where you begin at a distance and break the final behavior up into minute steps. Then, slowly and via a series of steps, the exposure to the "trigger" situation increases at a pace that the individual dog is comfortable with. When done properly, desensitization will help the dog to feel more comfortable overall with the processes.

Photo credit: Lara Oneschak

As discussed earlier, counter-conditioning can be explained as pairing a potentially unpleasant experience with a desirable one in order to change the animal's conditioned emotional response (CER).

In order to desensitize to grooming, you can use the process of desensitization to help the dog feel more comfortable with body-parts handling. As the grooming process often requires some physical manipulation, this would be a good place to begin. You can start by looking for calm and relaxed behavior.

This translates to a lack of tension in the muscles and no overt signs of stress. Outward and observable signs of stress would include such behaviors as: panting, lip licking, pulling or looking away, and, of course, growling, to name a few (see Chapter 3, Body Language).

Creating a positive Conditioned Emotional Response (CER)

Our goal with the grooming behavior chain is to create a positive conditioned emotional response. This means that the dog enjoys (or, at a minimum, tolerates with marginal discomfort) the visit to the groomer's. The dog's emotional state will be conveyed via observable and quantifiable behavior.

An example of a positive CER behavior chain is as follows.

The dog's guardian wakes up excited about taking his dog to the groomer's for a wonderful experience. The dog may sense this relaxed atmosphere, and wags his tail while displaying loose and wiggly body language in anticipation of departure from the house. Next, the dog and guardian would get in the car or walk to the grooming shop. As they near the shop, the dog would appear to be really eager, with more enthusiastic body language, and would perhaps even pull his guardian toward the shop, in hopes of a wonderful experience—their previous trips equaled comfortable handling and treats!

The groomer would come out to meet the dog, and the dog would respond with an animated greeting—the dog would squirm and strain to approach his "friend," He would then be taken into the grooming area and placed on the table where he would wait calmly and enjoy treats (perhaps from a "Chase 'n Chomp" pet chew toy: https://www.amazon.com/Chase-Chomp-Sticky-Bone-Chew/dp/B00D0S4MOY).

The groomer would then do the basics, and the dog would respond calmly via relaxed body language. Overall body handling, trimming, washing, and clipping would go smoothly and easily.

Next up would be nails. While nail clipping may have been a difficult and scary experience for the dog in the past, he now associates it with more treats and perhaps some breaks so that he can take a moment to relax in-between each nail being clipped. Ear cleaning would be the next step. The dog now associates ear manipulation with his favorite special treats, helping him to feel more positive about this experience. Then the pup would be ready for the next piece—being put in the tub. Once again, peanut butter or cream cheese on the side of the tub, along with a slow-paced process toward the final bath, has enabled the dog to no longer tremble during this step. Finally, towel drying equates to comfortable body handling, and the dog has learned to enjoy the treats and attention from the groomer with whom he is familiar and comfortable.

The blow dryer too, having been introduced slowly and over time, would no longer be scary, and so the dog might anticipate the next step—the haircut—without trepidation. Stationing on the table, once again with brief pauses for some control and choice in the process, has enabled the dog to feel empowered and relaxed throughout.

So what has occurred here is that each step in the process is reinforced by the next step in a positive manner, leading up to the dog's being returned to the guardian—as the final reinforcer.

Creating an Aversive Conditioned Emotional Response (CER)

Unfortunately, there is another version of this behavior chain that occurs frequently. Guardians, for whatever reason, may try out different groomers. They may notice, consciously or subconsciously, things happening on the day of the grooming that they don't particularly like. Perhaps they just don't like the haircut. Most likely, however, it is the dog's temperament and behavior as related to the groomer which has resulted in a less than optimal experience.

This is an example of the same scenario with a very different result. The dog's caregiver begins the day of the grooming with apprehension, thinking about having to drag the dog the last couple of blocks to the grooming shop. The dog may see the leash and other cues that indicate a trip to the grooming shop. He might immediately begin by backing up, spinning, and generally acting reluctant to head out the door. The owner, meanwhile, struggles to get the dog leashed, and then pulls the dog along. People are staring at them as they move along in this fashion, and the owner, out of embarrassment and/or frustration, might yell at the dog.

Upon arrival at the shop, people note the dog's apprehension and might try to help calm the dog down. The dog, however, is already stressed and not able to relax. In fact, the more that attempts are made to encourage calm with the stressed-out dog, the more stressed the dog becomes. Petting doesn't help, and, in fact, the dog may be frightened by hands approaching him, and may avert his eyes, lip lick, snarl, growl, or even snap. He won't accept any treats because he's already anorexic (refusing/unable to eat) and his system is full of cortisol as a result of the anxiety and stress.

The groomer comes out and takes the dog to the back of the shop. The dog is shaking, not focusing on the groomer, and continuing to stiffen up. The groomer starts to shave around the rectum while the dog resists this procedure by moving around because he's uncomfortable and anxious about being touched and physically manipulated. Meanwhile, the groomer is getting annoyed. Next, the groomer shaves the paw pads while the dog flails around and tries to communicate that he doesn't want his paws touched. Now the groomer holds the dog down, or has somebody else hold the dog down, in order to get this step done.

Next up is nail clipping. The dog moves his paws and pulls them back, perhaps even escalating to snapping or biting at the groomer. This, all the while, is making the nail clipping more difficult and much more time-consuming. The groomer might then call for an assistant to hold the dog's mouth or to muzzle the dog so as to be able to complete the nail clipping. Meanwhile, the dog is absolutely beside himself with fear, and with no relief in sight.

Finally, with the nails having been clipped, the dog now gets put in the bathtub. At this point, the dog is completely over threshold. Wanting to be anywhere but in the bathtub, the dog starts to move around, standing up in the tub, thrashing around, and generally making the bath very difficult. Once the bath is finished, the dog needs to be dried. The poor dog is already beside himself with stress and anxiety. He now begins snapping, he may be unable to stand still, or he may freeze or even begin cowering.

Since the dog is also frightened by sound of the dryer and the sensation of the air blowing over him, he flounders around, vocalizes, and makes several attempts to get away from the blow dryer. The dog's constant movement makes the drying process even longer and more uncomfortable for both groomer and dog.

At last the dog is dry and brushed out and ready for his haircut. The tactile sensation of the clipper blade on his body produces additional stress, so again; he's not standing still. The dog's bouncing up and down makes it very difficult and dangerous for the groomer to safely clip the legs. The groomer tries to scissor the legs, but it's still problematic to safely and effectively do this with a squirming animal. Finally, after trying to do a good job while avoiding injury to the dog, the body is clipped—and now the dog needs to get his face trimmed.

The dog has now become so stressed that he is in a constant state of movement. To avoid injuring the dog, the groomer grabs the dog's chin and moves the dog's head around, meanwhile grabbing the dog by its neck to stabilize it. This restraint further incites panic in the dog and he continues to thrash, snap, and bark. The groomer is relieved when the haircut is finally done.

The dog, meanwhile, is incredibly stressed and is not going to forget the awful experience he has just undergone. He's going to be reactive and nervous for a period of time after the grooming experience until the cortisol and other stress-creating neurotransmitters in his body have the chance to dissipate.

To top off the situation, the groomer is nervous about the grooming taking longer than it should have, and her boss is annoyed with her for taking so long. It has become a stressful situation for all.

We see the results of this type of over-threshold handling all the time with dogs that don't even want to walk down the same street where the shop is located. Their avoidance behavior demonstrates to us that they have found their prior grooming experiences to be extremely aversive. The good news, however, is that there are alternatives!

Solutions

Other, more modern, science-based choices can help! Options include gaining an understanding of what causes stress, how to tell if an animal is anxious, the signs to watch for when a dog is relaxed vs. frightened, and how to improve the experience and associated feelings and behaviors for a more positive outcome.

By learning to recognize the signs of stress, and respond appropriately we can build better relationships with our animal clients and their families. This, in turn, will help to improve upon the experience for you, your staff, the animals, and their guardians, which translates to a safer, more profitable, and less stressful grooming shop!

Although, hopefully, not every dog that passes through the shop each day puts groomers (and themselves) through the aversive scenario described above, we all know that similar occurrences take place too often at too many grooming shops. By committing to use the combined skills and techniques of desensitization, counter-conditioning and keen body language interpretation, you can work to avoid this second cycle of events wherein the methods used are largely to blame.

We have now established scenarios for both ends of the grooming continuum. On one end, we have each behavior in the chain being reinforced by the previous behavior, as well as treats being given throughout the process, all leading to a to a happy, cooperative dog. On the other end, we have each step in the same chain increasing the animal's stress level. In the latter scenario, the grooming trip takes longer, the dog learns right away that the grooming shop is a place where he's going to be uncomfortable, and you may not see this client return.

The goal of this book is to present different ways to make this long- duration behavior chain a positive, joyful, relaxing, and comfortable experience, such as described in the first scenario. Too, this great experience for our dogs can and will make your grooming business stand out as a first-rate value in your area.

Crating comfort

Dogs may often need to be crated before or after being groomed. Teaching a dog to voluntarily enter a crate is a great skill. This can ensure that the dog is comfortable and safe in a variety of situations and settings, including the grooming shop. If we teach dogs to enter the crate voluntarily, they will be participating cooperatively in their care, which will help to alleviate stress and anxiety.

Engaging families to assist with crate training can help dogs feel much more comfortable when they need to be crated at the groomer's. Following is a plan that groomers can share with families to encourage them to work on this behavior at home, which will ultimately translate to safer, calmer dogs when needing to be in crates at your shop. You might even consider doing a small demo for families. Remember, extras such as a brief lesson help build relationships that can go a long way toward establishing trust and realizing the goal of a regular clientele and long-term grooming care.

Sample Training Plan: Crate Training

1. Click or use your verbal marker "yes" and treat for the dog looking at the crate.
2. Toss a couple of high-value treats into the crate and leave the door open.
3. Allow the dog to move in and out of the crate.
4. Click (or use your verbal marker "yes") and treat for the dog choosing to go into the crate. Do not close the door.
5. Continue clicking and treating for any interaction with the crate (choosing to look at it, choosing to go toward it, choosing to step in, choosing to go inside).
6. The next step is to close the door, once the dog is inside, and then immediately reopen it.
7. Click and treat for a calm, relaxed dog.

Tip: *You might consider sharing some body language examples with your clients via photos (Lili Chin has some very helpful drawings) to demonstrate the difference between relaxed and stressed dogs.*

Photo credit: Laura Arlene Miller

Continue building duration in the crate and clicking and treating for the dog remaining calm inside. At the same time, you should also randomly alternate closing the door for a very short time, then re-opening it, with closing it for a bit longer duration before re-opening. Click and treat for calm behavior.

This process will likely take several sessions for it to be successful. Depending upon the individual dog, it may go more or less quickly. As such, partnering with the guardian(s) to work on this skill at home will be of great help to the groomer, and your suggesting this to them is strongly recommended.

8 MODERN GROOMING PRACTICES

All throughout the animal world, from zoos to aquariums to shelters, interactions are moving in the direction of training for voluntary cooperation of husbandry behaviors. This means that we want the animal to actively tolerate, if not happily participate in, behaviors that involve its care. Grooming is one such behavior.

The first step would be to discuss how we actually develop cooperative behaviors. Do we take a one-size-fits-all approach? Or do we customize a plan for each animal?

Relationship-Building

Your relationship with the dog is always the most important thing to consider. All other factors will stem from this key point. Whether you are the animal's family, caregiver, veterinarian, trainer, or groomer, each person who interacts with the animal will have a relationship with that animal. We want to be sure that we foster and promote that relationship in a positive way.

We all want to keep and build repeat business and have regular customers who come every four to six weeks for their haircuts. The frequency of these visits offers a unique opportunity for relationship-building as well as a steady workflow. To that end, we want to think of relationship-building as an extremely important part of each visit.

You want the dog to like you, and you want the guardian to trust you. In order to be successful, you want to develop and build a marketing strategy that includes this relationship-building at the center of everything else that you do. Teaching cooperative behaviors and shaping them is a big part of this plan. Another key element is building those personal relationships with the guardians that are largely based on trust concerning their dogs' safety, well-being, happiness, and comfort at the grooming shop.

Shaping

A key component in the process of building and developing a positive, trusting relationship is via a skill called, "shaping." According to Karen Pryor (clickertraining.com/node/1135), "The word 'shaping' is scientific slang for building a particular behavior by using a series of small steps to achieve it."

Once we've committed to shaping these skills, we need to understand just how to go about this task successfully. The following are Karen Pryor's updated principles which clarify the key shaping components.

Photo credit: Kota Oliver with Frannie Mae

1. **Be prepared before you start.** Be ready to reinforce behavior that you like right from the very first interaction. When shaping a new behavior, be ready to capture the very first tiny inclination the animal gives you toward your goal behavior. Example: Have your tools, treats, and space all set up before you begin. This way if the dog sniffs the clippers you are ready with a yummy treat!

2. **Ensure success at each step.** Break behavior down into small enough pieces that the learner always has a realistic chance to earn a reinforcer. In other words, be ready to

reinforce anything that you like and want to see repeated! Example: If you would like the dog to calmly interact with the clippers, you might start by giving him a tiny treat for even just glancing at them without any signs of stress.

3. **Train one criterion at a time.** Shaping for two criteria or aspects of a behavior simultaneously can be very confusing. Decide upon your criteria and make it easy to achieve. Example: Let's say that you want the dog to look at you and stand calmly. Begin with just the "look at you" portion and later focus on the second half of your criteria (stand calmly)!

4. **Relax criteria when something changes.** When introducing a new criterion or aspect of the skill, temporarily relax the old criteria for previously mastered skills. Example: If as in the previous example, you want the dog do look at you and stand calmly, once you begin working on the second half (stand calmly) you might be ok with the dog providing just intermittent eye contact vs. consistently keeping eye contact—then building back towards the constant eye contact once you have them standing calmly, too!

5. **If one door closes, find another.** If a particular shaping procedure is not progressing, try another way. Example: Let's say that you are trying to shape the dog to move calmly towards the clippers on the table. Maybe this isn't working and you need to try it with peanut butter on the clippers on the ground first!

6. **Keep training sessions continuous.** The animal should be continuously engaged in the learning process throughout the session. He should be working the entire time, except for the moment he's consuming/enjoying his reinforcer. This also means keeping a high rate of reinforcement. Example: In a 20 second session you might want to count out 10 treats. This will help you to remember to watch for things that you like and to reinforce them often!

7. **Go back to kindergarten, if necessary.** If a behavior deteriorates, quickly revisit the last successful approximation or two so that the animal can easily earn reinforcers. Example: If you are working on the dog offering his paw to you for a nail trim and suddenly he's acting stressed about this, you might need to take a step or two backwards. Will he allow you to touch his paw with just one finger lightly? If yes, begin there and build back up to an offered paw in your hand!

8. **Keep your attention on your learner.** Interrupting a training session gratuitously by taking a phone call, chatting, or doing something else that can wait often cause learners to lose momentum and get frustrated by the lack of information. Example: If you need to take a break, give the animal a "goodbye present," such as a small handful of treats.

9. **Stay ahead of your learner.** Be prepared to "skip ahead" in your shaping plan if your learner makes a sudden leap.

Example: If the dog that you are working with is relaxed while you touch his paws, you may be able to move a bit faster and touch the clippers to the nail in the first session.

10. **Quit while you're ahead.** End each session with something the learner finds reinforcing. If possible, end a session with a strong behavioral response, but, at any rate, try to end with your learner still eager to go on. Example, if you are working on teaching the dog to remain stationary on the table, try to practice for 1 minute, then 1 minute 30 seconds. The temptation may be to continue to increase your duration, however "quitting while you are ahead" means to take a break once you are successful and to come back at the issue again in another session!

Using these principles in a "real life scenario" might proceed as follows below. The second principle, to ensure success at each step, focuses on shaping in increments in such a way that the dog has a reasonable chance of being successful. What exactly does this mean, and how do we do it? Let's take a look at how this applies to three types of dog clients.

First is the "brand new puppy" client. This is a dog that will be coming to your shop on a regular basis and that you might find very challenging to handle. Second is the "new client," who has arrived at your shop via word of mouth and your good reputation. Finally, the third type of client is the one that arrives at your door as a dog that is "frightened and terrified" of the grooming process.

With the new puppy, you have an opportunity to create a positive conditioned emotional response from the start. Puppies are naturally curious and, depending on the puppy's age, may be still in the ever-important socialization period (up to 12-14 weeks). As such, we suggest that you move very slowly. Do your Meet and Treat, and then work on making positive associations and first impressions. Offer the puppy safe choices such as the opportunity to sniff and investigate, or the chance to approach you and other "new" things in the shop, vs the other way around. Keep your session short and relaxed. With the next dog, your "walk-in new client," you also want to be sure that there are many opportunities for the dog to investigate at a pace that is comfortable for him, and that he has a pleasant experience with both you and the location. Once more, allow this dog to come to you—remember to avoid direct eye contact, and consider crouching down and facing sideways when safe to do so. Watch for wiggly body language (good!) and see if the new dog will take treats from you. This is valuable information about his anxiety level. Also, suggest to the caregiver that the first visit is a "shop intro," aka Meet and Treat (see chapter 3). Then, use this time to help the dog to begin to feel more relaxed with you and your venue, after which you can set up an appointment for a return visit – which automatically buys you more time to slowly help the dog feel more comfortable.

The third dog is one who arrives stressed and anxious. There is great potential here to really help this dog get through the process uninjured (both dog *and* groomer) and in a reasonably calm state so as not to affect your relationship in a negative way. You want to keep in mind that the families of this type of dog will also be spreading the word about how you were able to transform their dog's reaction to being groomed—from frightened and uncooperative to relaxed and compliant. Let's say that this dog has only been handled via traditional methods in the past (we refer here to methods that do not necessarily take into consideration the comfort and feedback of the dog). In the next chapter we will detail an initial shaping plan in small increments for target training with a target stick that you could use for the Meet and Treat with this type of client.

9 SKILLS

In this section we will look at training a set of behaviors and skills that will help dogs to feel more confident and comfortable with the grooming process. We can break most skills down into two categories: targeting and stationing. Basically, we want to teach dogs what it is that we would like them to do (targeting) and where we want them to be (stationing).

Target Training

Targeting helps to give the dog something specific to do, which we can then reinforce. Targeting is a great building-block behavior. It works on focus and confidence building. Additionally, targeting behaviors are incompatible with, or are an alternative to, other less-desirable behaviors. The concept is to teach a dog to touch a part of his body to a target, which can be a hand (if there isn't a bite risk) or a target stick. A target stick is generally a long wand with a ball at the end. However, a long-handled spoon or spatula can work as well! Targeting teaches the animal that it can choose to touch the target and earn access to something that it finds reinforcing. In other words, if the animal decides to touch the target, it gets something that it likes—which, in this case, is most likely a treat. As there is no force or physical manipulation in targeting, the animal has a choice, which can be quite empowering. It is also a great alternative behavior to teach, as opposed to a less desirable one (example: bite at the brush). The following is a plan for teaching a dog to target.

Sample training plan: Target Stick

To get started with target-stick training you'll need a target stick of some kind and some high-value treats. In this sample training plan you will teach the dog to touch his nose to the ball of the target stick (or the end of the stick substitute):

1. Touch the ball end of the target stick to something that smells interesting (like tuna), and place it about a half-inch from the front of the dog's nose.
2. When the dog naturally brings his nose to the ball, mark (click or use your verbal marker "yes") at the exact moment that the dog's nose touches the ball, and then treat.
3. Repeat Step 2 again. Once you have the dog heading to the ball easily, no longer "dip" the ball end but continue to mark and reinforce nose touches to the ball.
4. After the dog is consistently touching his nose to the ball of the target stick, you can increase the difficulty level by starting to move the target stick around a bit. Try holding it a couple of inches to the left of the dog's face. Remember to keep it easy enough for the dog to "get it correct" as you slowly make it more challenging.

Tip: *If the dog does not touch the target within three seconds, remove your target, but then immediately bring it back into position for another try. After two tries, if the dog does not touch the target, drop back to an easier level (perhaps the one where your target has the "tuna smell") and do a few repetitions there before moving to the more challenging level again.*

Sample Training Plan: Hand Target

With this sample training plan you will be teaching the dog to touch his nose to your hand as the target. Be sure to use this plan only when you are sure that the dog feels relaxed about your hand near his face.

For this plan you will need some high-value treats and a dog.

1. Put a small treat in your hand and close it into a fist around the food, then place your closed hand about a half-inch in front of the dog's nose.
2. When the dog naturally brings his nose to your fist, mark (click or use your verbal marker "yes") at the exact moment that the dog's nose touches your fist; open it and give the dog the treat. Repeat this step a few times in a row.
3. Then present your closed hand (fist) without a treat inside, and when the dog brings his nose to your fist, mark (click or use your verbal marker "yes") at the exact

moment that the dog's nose touches your fist – then get a treat and give it to the dog. Repeat this step a few times in a row.
4. Next, place your open palm hand (hint: be sure that your hand is positioned with palm facing the dog's nose and held there firmly in place as it is the "target") about a half-inch from the dog's nose.
5. When the dog brings his nose to your hand, mark (click or use your verbal marker "yes") at the exact moment that the dog's nose touches your open palm – then get a treat and give to the dog.

Tip: *If the dog does not touch within three seconds, remove your hand, but then immediately bring it back into position for another try. After two tries, if the dog does not touch the hand, drop back to an easier level and do a few repetitions before moving up to the open-hand target again.*

After the dog learns to target a target stick and/or a hand target, with all of the above steps in mind, you may use any tool in your grooming toolbox as a target. For example, you could have the dog practice targeting the clippers or a brush. In this way, it can also help to make the tools less "scary," as they predict something good occurring when the dog chooses to get close to them!

Stationing

As noted at the beginning of this chapter, the concept of stationing teaches a dog where we would like him to be. Stationing, therefore, is when we teach a dog to remain in position in a certain spot. This is a handy behavior as you may often need your dog to station on the table while grooming, or while in his cubby waiting for his turn, or when finished.

Photo credit: Anna Day with Theo

We can teach a dog to station in place by making the behavior reinforcing. Let's say that each time you sat in a certain chair you were handed a one hundred dollar bill. It is likely that you might find the money reinforcing and associate it with the chair. Therefore, it is also likely that you might choose to sit in that chair more frequently. We'll be teaching the dog the same concept via training a stationing behavior.

Sample Training Plan: Stationing
To start, you will need some high-value treats. If using a clicker as a marker, you'll want to have this on hand as well. Remember you can also use a verbal marker instead.

1. Begin by placing a treat where you would like the dog to be.
2. Ask for a sit or a down in the location where you would like the dog to be, and then mark (click or use your verbal marker "yes") and reinforce if the dog responds appropriately.
3. Rock back on your heels, and if the dog remains in place, immediately mark (click or use your verbal marker "yes"), and then return to the dog to reinforce.
4. After rocking a couple of times, and marking and reinforcing the lack of movement, take one step back. Immediately mark (click or use your verbal marker "yes") if the dog does not move, and return to the dog to reinforce.
5. Continue building this behavior slowly, and at some

distance, always marking and reinforcing for the dog remaining in place.

6. If the dog moves, back up a step or two to make it easier for the dog to get it "correct," and when he does, be sure to mark (click or use your verbal marker "yes") and reinforce.

7. You can also (slowly) add in some distractions. For example you might pick up a brush or scissors (but not move them towards the dog at the start). Again, mark and reinforce remaining in place.

Tip: *At the beginning, you will want to provide frequent feedback (in the form of marking and reinforcing) so that the dog understands the message that staying in place is worthwhile!*

To apply the concept of stationing to the grooming table, place the dog on the table and follow the steps above. Immediately treat for standing on all four paws without movement, even if it's only a second. Then remove the dog from the table. Place the dog back on the table and play the "game" again.

You will want to repeat this cycle in order to get a high rate of reinforcement going, and turn it into a fun "game." The high rate of reinforcement comes about from the frequency with which you are marking (clicking or using your verbal marker "yes") and reinforcing. As such, be sure to keep doing this every second or so!

Next, you can build some duration for the on-table stationing and standing behavior by "yo-yo-ing" the length of time that you ask the dog to remain still. That is, you might do one step with one second, then mark/reinforce. The next step might be five or ten seconds (depending on what you have been able to work up to as far as duration), and then mark/reinforce, followed by a last step of two seconds, then mark/reinforce.

At this point, you might also use your treat delivery to enable you to begin to examine the dog. That is, once you have the dog standing on the table, waiting for his treat, give him the treat and start to palpate and examine the dog so you can begin your grooming process. If you have the time, continue to allow the dog to be comfortable just standing relaxed on the table, and be sure to reinforce this nice, relaxed behavior.

Targeting and Stationing

Now you can practice putting the two skills together to continue to build nice table behaviors for grooming. You can also build duration for the stationing behavior by using the "hand Kong" (a term coined by Jay Andors, co-author). Simply put something tasty in your closed fist and ask the dog to target it while standing still—at first, for just a second—then open your hand and allow the dog to eat. Gradually work on extending the amount of time that you would like the dog to remain still, in place; however, remember to "bounce" between shorter and longer durations so that the difficulty level isn't always increasing, which could risk the dog's becoming frustrated.

Next, take the dog off the table and restock your hand once more with something tempting. Then put the pup back on the table and, keeping your fist closed, allow the dog to investigate your hand for two or three seconds. While the dog is standing still on all four paws, open your hand to allow him to eat. Then take him off the table and repeat the steps. This is a way of using luring (food in hand) and targeting (dog touching nose to "hand Kong") simultaneously while working on making stationing (remaining comfortably in one spot) reinforcing to the dog.

10 TOOLS

We have already discussed the principles of desensitization and counter-conditioning, and how they would apply to specific situations regarding the clippers, blow dryer, etc. Should you encounter a situation during your grooming process where an animal feels stressed, just creatively apply those principles by associating what is scary with something yummy and moving at a pace that the dog demonstrates he feels comfortable with.

Blow Dryer

There are several factors to consider with regard to helping the dog feel comfortable with the blow dryer in the shop.
1. noise
2. stabilize
3. tactile (forced air on different body parts)

Let's break down each of these components a bit. We want to be cognizant of the fact that some dogs can be highly sound-sensitive, and blow drying can be a very frightening part of the grooming experience. We also want to consider the feel of forced air on different parts of the body that can evoke fear if this is a new experience. Finally, depending on the temperament, size, physical challenges, and age of the dog, the best way to stabilize him during this process will vary.

Stabilizing a dog for drying can be done in a few different ways. The Groomer's Helper might be a good aid for this type of situation. If your dog is old and can't stand up, products like this may come in handy. The Groomer's Helper has an arm that can be placed under the dog's belly to act as a support. Remember, it is always important to make sure that the dog is comfortable with the support and any other apparatus being used (like the blow dryer). Yet another option is to just support the dog with your arm. When working with a puppy, you can simply hold the pup in your lap, first making sure the dog is comfortable with the sound of the dryer and the tactile sensation of the air against his body.

Blow drying, force drying, or fluff drying are terms given to the process of drying the dog after it has been bathed. Unlike human hair, a dog's hair should be dry and clean in order for it to be cut properly. It takes time for this process to be completed, as the more perfectly dry and fluffed out a dog is, the more even the cut will be. Blow drying, force drying, or fluff drying are terms given to the process of drying the dog after it has been bathed.

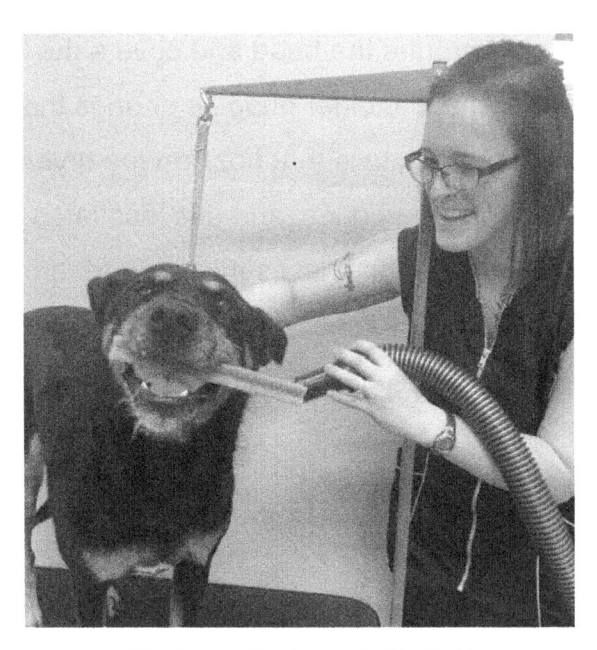

Photo credit: Amanda Hatfield

It takes time for this process to be completed, as the more perfectly dry and fluffed out a dog is, the more even the cut will be. This will, of course, depend on the skill of the groomer as well. (Anne Francis, a co-author of this book, has had several good articles on this in regard to a variety of specialized cuts in *Grooming Business* magazine.) For an older dog that has lost his hearing, drying may not be a problem; however, he may still retain some anxiety from previous experiences. Sometimes, older dogs actually like the tactile sensation of the air pressure on their bodies.

Another tool that can be helpful in this situation is the "Happy Hoodie." The Happy Hoodie is a round, stretchy piece of material that goes around the head and covers the ears. It may often be of benefit to older puppies or dogs that appear nervous. Also good to note is that nozzle-type dryers are less noisy than the flat-shaped ones, and use less force with air. One more tip is to begin on a low setting; some force-driers have one or two motor switches, or a dial, to adjust the strength of the air.

When drying, we suggest that you start at the rear so that the dog has more time to get used to the feel of the blower. Sometimes the sound of the dryer may cause an elderly dog to have a mini-seizure. If you find yourself in a situation where the dog barks uncontrollably, this is a potentially dangerous situation, and you should stop the blower immediately and calm the dog. We advise to carefully observe the dog's body language during the drying process so that you can promptly intervene way before this can happen.

Stress signs to watch for include excessive barking, a change in the sound of the bark (such as a high-pitched bark), and/or excessive struggling. First, you might see the dog trying to get away from the flow of air coming from the dryer. Rather than allowing the situation to escalate, stop immediately and change your plan to either an air-dry or cage-dry option. It's never worth potentially causing a seizure or a "scary" experience that would only make future similar situations more aversive and anxiety-provoking. Remember, the most important goal is to work with the dog *below* his threshold level of comfort, in order to avoid even more serious issues in the future.

A good blow dryer will usually have different settings, so it's important to choose the one that's right for each particular dog. Remember that the dryers are very noisy, and noise can be extremely stressful. This is especially true if an animal is highly sensitive to sound.

Another option for drying is to dry the dog in the kennel ("cage drying"). In this case, the drying is done with no heat and only utilizes recycled room-temperature air. This can be done if the dog is comfortable in the cage. If opting to dry the dog in the kennel, keep in mind that it's very important to continually monitor the dog, especially in the summer months. Most states now have laws regarding using heat in cages, as they can become ovens very quickly. For this reason, we recommend using no heat at all, and switching settings to just cool air. The drying process may take longer, but it's a much safer way to go, especially in very busy shops.

Speaking of busy shops, there are grooming shops that do a large volume of dogs. The shop employees often make use of cages and cage dryers. Dog guardians should always inquire about this. We recommend asking if your dog will be put in a cage dryer and if heat will be used! There have been deaths in recent years as a result of dogs placed in cage dryers with heat and lack of monitoring. We suggest that you insist that your dog not be put in a cage that has a dryer using a heat setting. This is a major safety concern, and should be top priority to confirm.

If the dog is fearful of both blow drying and cage drying, rather than risk creating more serious associations for the dog at future visits, we recommend allowing the dog to air dry, and just brushing him out once completely dry. If the dog is too panicked, we'd suggest waiting until he is able to calm down, and then have the guardian take him home and bring him back the next day or so to finish the cut.

Once more, the key here is the future behavior and associations that you are trying to create and protect. Pushing beyond the dog's threshold now—to get the job done—can only cause trouble for the next time. A much better option is to stop and break the process up, so that moving forward, the dog is more comfortable and things will be safer and speedier. Thinking about the "long game" is a win-win for dogs, human clients, and groomers/other shop employees.

Sample training plan: Blow Dryer and Grooming Shop

Sounds Desensitization

1. This first step in the plan for new puppy families should be to play a recording of blowers from the grooming shop (you can record this sound on your cell phone).
2. Then, while comfortably at home, guardians should play the sounds loud at various times (perhaps while the dog is feeding or just resting) and click and treat for calm behavior. While this is only an introduction to the potential stress of a blow dryer, and not a substitute for duration and other possible sounds and smells that may add stress when in the shop, it is a good plan with which to begin the desensitization process.

Tip: *A good place for the sounds to be played at home is in an area like the bathroom where there will be an echo that will mirror some of the bathing and blowing sounds that the dog will experience in some areas of the shop. Safety note: Be sure you aren't using an actual dryer near a tub filled with water in the bathroom.*

3. Next, play the sounds while brushing the dog. You will want to stop periodically to click and treat for calm behavior. A high rate of reinforcement is recommended here, so every twenty seconds, click and treat for calm. This practice will help to simulate fluff drying. Be sure to click and treat for calm behavior throughout this activity.
4. Now continue while actually using a household blow dryer. If your household doesn't happen to have a blow

dryer, it may be a good investment for these home practice sessions as well as for touch-ups on the dog's' hair post rainy-day walks.

These sound simulations can go a long way toward helping to desensitize the animal to the sounds it will encounter in the grooming shop. Be sure to always click and treat for calm behavior.

Sample Training Plan: Blow Dryer at the Grooming Shop

1. With the dog on the table, click and treat for calm behavior. Repeat this a few times (maybe five to eight times in a row).
2. Place the dryer, in the off position, away from (and pointing away from) the dog. Click and treat for the dog being near the dryer and remaining calm.
3. If the dog has previously had a bad/scary experience with the dryer, he may not be able to remain relaxed when close to it. In this case, an interim step would be to move the dryer further away (continuing to move it further and further away until the dog is relaxed), and click and treat for calm. Once the dog is calm, you would slowly (maybe only six inches at a time) move the dryer closer, then stop and click and treat for the dog remaining calm.
4. Next, turn the dryer on and immediately off again. Click

and treat for calm. If the dog becomes stressed with the dryer on and close by, turn it off and add an interim step of moving it away again, and then turning it back on. You would repeat the steps of moving it closer (now, while on) and clicking and treating for the dog remaining calm.

5. Turn the dryer on and leave it on for a few seconds (maybe three to five seconds) and then turn it off. Click and treat for calm.
6. Turn the dryer on. While on, click and treat for the dog remaining calm and relaxed.
7. Move the dryer closer and repeat numbers 4 through 6.
8. Move the dryer away again and point it at the dog. Repeat numbers 4 through 6.
9. Move the dryer closer (a little at a time if necessary) and move it over different parts of the dog's body. Click and treat for calm behavior.

If at any time the dog begins to show signs of anxiety and stress, back up to an "easier" step where the dog was relaxed. You may also need to stop and repeat this process by breaking it up into more than one session.

Be careful not to practice this activity for longer than a total of five minutes. Then, depending on the dog's level of nervousness, you can make a judgment call about when you feel the dog is ready to be groomed. For example, some dogs may benefit by having the guardian bring the dog to the shop two or three times, if possible, before the actual grooming begins.

If having the dog make multiple visits to the shop prior to actually using the blow dryer on him is not possible, and you need to dry the dog, try to expose him to the dryer in small increments throughout the day, using it on him for just a couple of minutes at a time and clicking and treating for calm behavior.

The bather can also assist by brushing out the dog while the blower is on and treating for calm behavior; this also helps in building a relationship with the dog and bather.

Tip: *Ideally, there would be treats accessible in different areas around the shop so that all members of the staff can regularly treat to reinforce calm behavior. Always check with owners in case of specialized diets or allergies.*

Note that if the dog is uncomfortable getting blow-dried, and comes in with very long hair that is not matted, it's a good idea to rough-cut the dog prior to bathing it.

By going slowly, and at a pace that the dog can handle, we can succeed in transforming the dryer from a scary tool into one that predicts good things. In this way, we help the dog to feel comfortable with the dryer, which, going forward, means a faster, easier, and safer process for everyone!

The Groomer's Helper

Another tool that you can help your client dogs feel more comfortable with is the Groomer's Helper. Our goal is here is collaborative restraint. The following plan can guide you through the steps to ensure that the dogs you work with are more relaxed with this groom shop staple.

Sample training plan: Groomer's Helper

Before beginning, be sure that the dog is relaxed and comfortable. Have plenty of tiny (smaller than a dime), high-value, soft and tasty treats on hand (Examples of small, soft commercial treats which work well are Zukes or Pet Botanics).

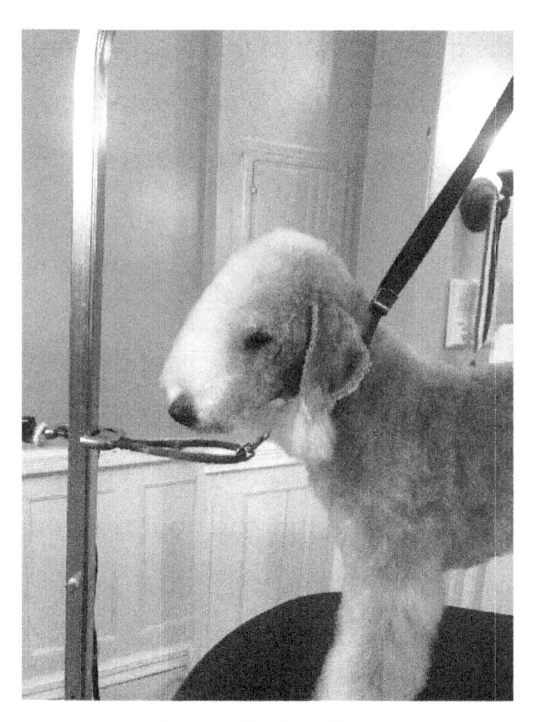

Photo credit: Eric Chassey

1. Place the dog on the table and click (or use your verbal marker word) and treat for calm.
2. Click and treat for the dog looking at or sniffing the objects/apparatus that make up the Groomer's Helper.
3. Move the apparatus closer and closer to the dog as long as the dog remains relaxed. If the dog is calm, click and treat. This helps to make good associations with the sight and smell of the apparatus—in this case, the "grooming loop" part.
4. Click and treat for any calm behavior. If the dog shows signs of stress, remove him from the table and take a break.

5. Once the dog is off the table, unhook the main collar, present it to the dog, and allow the dog to sniff it. Click, or use your verbal marker "yes," and treat for the dog calmly sniffing the collar.
6. Repeat this process until the dog is comfortable in the presence of the collar.

Tip: *As a side note, the process of making sure that the dog is relaxed around the collar should be done with all dogs before you put any collars on them.*

7. If the dog is reluctant to allow you to put the collar over his head, we can then move to shape calm behavior for this part of the process. The way this works would be to present the collar loop directly in front of the dog's face, and then, if the dog is calm, click or use the verbal marker word and then offer a treat in such a way that the dog has to put his head through the collar loop. If putting his head through the loop is too "difficult" for a first step, just calmly click and treat for the initial sniffing and exploring of the loop. You may need to repeat this step several times before the dog becomes comfortable. Then place the dog back up onto the table. You can also repeat this process on the table.
8. Once the collar is on the dog, the next step is to hook it back up to the grooming arm. Be careful with this step: if

the dog were to panic at this point (he might feel trapped), the collar could become very frightening and aversive. If the dog becomes stressed, you will want to back up a few steps and only continue to proceed once the dog can calmly stand on the table while wearing the Groomer's Helper attached to the table arm.

9. Next, take the cord with the clip that's attached to the device and attach it to the loop under the dog's neck (this is a good feature of the apparatus that prevents you from inadvertently choking the dog) Click and treat for the dog remaining still in this position.

10. Remove the loop from around the dog's neck and take a brief break. Repeat these steps until the dog is comfortable, clicking and treating for calm behavior.

11. Once you reach the point at which you can calmly place the groomer's loop gently over the dog's head (click and treat for calm), and also gently attach the Groomer's Helper (again, click and treat for calm), you should spend a minute clicking and treating (one treat follows each click) for the dog remaining calmly in place.

12. You might want to hang a lickety stick, a Chase and Chomp Sticky Bone, a bully stick, or something similar, that the dog can reach and focus on while you're doing the rear of the dog. This works as a distraction and also helps provide a positive association with the position and process.

13. Now you might clip around the dog's rectum and in-between the dog's paw pads.
14. Then unclip the dog, remove the loop, and take the dog off the table and release him so he can have a brief break.
15. Place the dog back on the table and click and treat for calmly remaining on the table while you again fit the loop over his head and attach the Groomer's Helper arm.

Tip: *Set up the Groomer's Helper before the dog arrives. Remember to treat for the dog looking at the objects that make up the Groomer's Helper or showing interest by calmly sniffing them. Too, be sure to click and treat for any other relaxed behavior. Also remember that if the dog shows signs of stress, remove him from the table, take a break, and then build the behavior up again slowly, starting with the easiest steps and/or the last step where the dog was relaxed.*

Decide ahead of time which part of the dog you are going to groom first. We suggest always starting at the back end, being the part furthest away from the dog's teeth. You will want to keep in mind that if you plan to immobilize the head, it's very important to remember to not keep it immobile throughout the entire grooming process. Stop and give the dog several short breaks. Plenty of breaks help the dog realize that it won't need to be in a position for too lengthy an amount of time, which should make the process less stressful.

Tip: *Families could help at home by practicing slipping something similar to a grooming loop over the dog's head and then clicking (or using a verbal marker) and treating for a calm reaction. They could work towards a longer duration (more time between click/treats for remaining calm) and begin to practice in a variety of locations around the house. This protocol also involves a stationing behavior, which is something that could be practiced at home as well (described in more detail in stationing plan in Chapter 10). Taking time to show clients how to practice these behaviors at home could constitute a free or paid-for lesson which will ultimately help the dog to feel more relaxed and happy about the grooming experience.*

If this is the first time for the loop and Groomer's Helper at the shop, and the dog is extremely agitated, the recommendation would be to break this behavior down and practice the loop, positioning, and stationing separately, either in the shop (valuable time paid for by the guardian) or at home. As noted above, the groomer could even charge for a mini-training lesson to instruct the family how to go about working on helping their dog practice at home.

Photo credit: Lindsey Dicken

Clippers

Another tool the owners can also help to desensitize to at home is the clippers. They don't necessarily need electric clippers to assist, but rather can use a hand-held massager or electric toothbrush to simulate the noise and vibration sensation. Be sure to share the plan below with clients who might want to try to help with practice at home so that their dog may feel more comfortable in the shop. Coaching owners on how to go about desensitization and counter-conditioning—

so that they don't inadvertently use flooding instead—can go a long way toward progress in the shop.

Sample Training Plan: Electric Clipper Desensitization

Before beginning, be sure that the dog is relaxed and comfortable. Also have electric clippers and high-value (according to the dog) treats with you.

1. With the dog on the table, click and treat for calm behavior. Repeat this a few times (five to eight) in a row.
2. Hold the clippers at arm's length away from the dog. Click and treat for the dog being near the clippers. If the dog has previously had a bad/scary experience with clippers, he may not be able to remain relaxed when close to them. In this case, an interim step would be to hold the clippers further away (and continue to move them further and further until the dog is calm), and click and treat for calm. Once the dog is calm, you would slowly (maybe even only six inches at a time) move the clippers closer, then stop and click and treat for the dog remaining calm.
3. Once the dog is able to remain relaxed on the table with the clippers close by in your hand, try touching the clippers (while still in the "off" position) to the dog's fur. Click and treat for calm behavior.
4. Next, holding the clippers away from the dog, turn them on and immediately off. Click and treat for calm.

5. Again, holding the clippers a bit away from the dog, turn them on and leave them on for a few seconds (five to eight) and then turn them off. Click and treat for calm.
6. Turn the clippers on. While on, click and treat the dog for remaining calm and relaxed.
7. Slowly move the clippers closer to the dog and click for calm. If necessary, repeat Steps 4 through 6.
8. Slowly move the clippers closer (a little at a time, as necessary) and use them briefly (just a few seconds to start with) on the dog. Click and treat for calm behavior.
9. If the dog is able to remain calm, continue using the clippers and treating often for relaxed behavior (every three seconds at the very beginning, and then stretching out this time between treats).

If, at any time, the dog begins to show signs of anxiety and stress, back up to an "easier" step (when the dog was relaxed and calm). You may also need to stop and repeat this process by breaking it up into more than one session. By going slowly, and at a pace that the dog can handle, we can succeed in transforming the clippers from a scary tool into one that predicts good things. In this way, we help the dog to feel comfortable with the clippers, which, going forward, means a faster, easier, and safer process for all!

11 SPECIALTY TECHNIQUES:

Hand-Stripping and Systematic Desensitization

As discussed in detail in Chapter 3 in order to help dogs feel more comfortable about scary or potentially scary situations, we will use a process called "desensitization." Systematic desensitization is a technique that was originally developed by psychologists to treat people with anxiety and phobias. The subject is exposed to a fear-provoking object or situation at an intensity that does not produce any response. If you are terrified of spiders, for example, your first hierarchy rung (first exposure) might involve showing you a cartoon of a friendly looking spider. You might even first look at this picture from a distance. If you are not at all anxious or afraid at this point, then you are going slowly enough in your approach and you are on the right track. The intensity—in this case, "degree of realism and proximity"—is very gradually increased, contingent upon the subject continuing to feel okay. A hierarchy is developed at the beginning of treatment, ranging from the easiest to most difficult versions of exposure to the stimulus.

As with all of the training plans discussed in this book, it's up to you as the groomer to start at the point where there is no reaction (fear), and then gradually build upon the procedure, at a rate at which the individual dog continues to be able to remain relaxed, while reinforcing the dog's calm behavior.

The process of hand-stripping, if not done in a way that allows the dog to feel comfortable, may be a very aversive procedure. As such, it is of great importance to discuss in minute detail here in order to fully appreciate the great care that should go into making hand-stripping as comfortable an experience as possible for the dog. In this regard, the most important thing that we want to focus on are the steps taken to ensure that the dog becomes accustomed and generalized to having his wiry outer coat being pulled out all over his body.

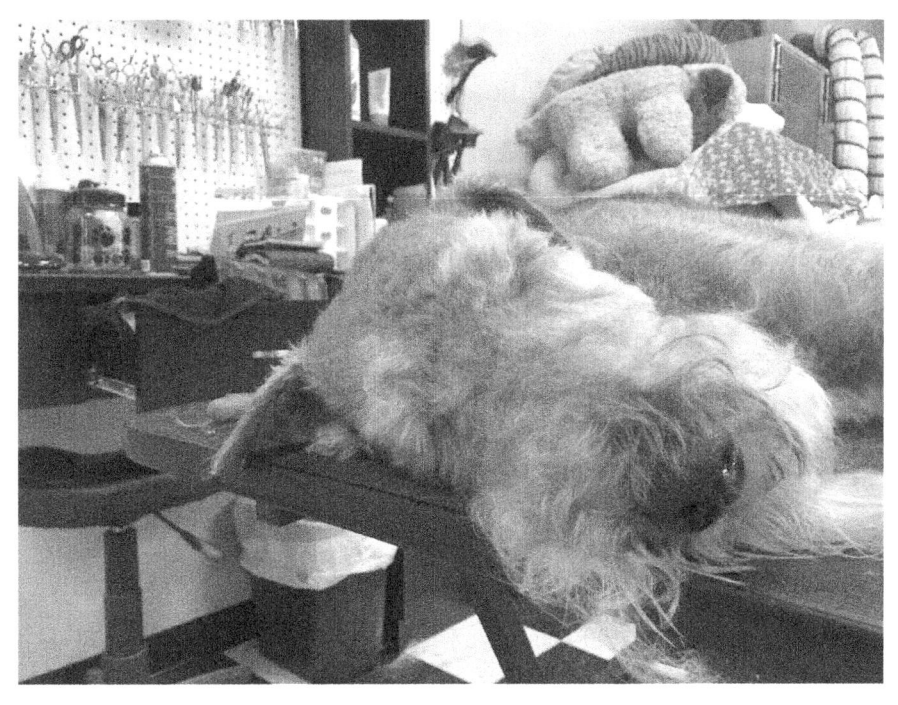

Photo credit: Christina Lorton Duncan

According to Wikipedia, ". . . hand-stripping is the process of pulling the dead hair out of the coat of a non-shedding dog, either by using a stripping knife or the fingers. A hard, wiry coat has a cycle where it starts growing and then sheds as it reaches maximum length. Hand-stripping coordinates the shedding and makes room for a new coat to grow."

Stripping is the proper grooming method for all wirehaired terriers, including Cairn Terriers, Fox Terriers, German White-Haired Pointers, Jack Russell Terriers, Schnauzers, Wirehaired Dachshunds, Wirehaired Pointing Griffons, West Hyland White Terriers, Border Terriers, and Bouvier des Flandres. All show dogs must be hand-stripped all over, whereas with pet dogs, you can simulate the look of hand-stripping by using a thinning shears. However, the area of the coat that has been cut with shears will lose its hardness, so it is a choice to consider when picking your tools and planning your cut. As such, when at all possible, it is best to shape the dog to comfortably tolerate hand-stripping all over its body.

The hair is removed either by bracing it against a stripping knife or a stripping stone (volcanic rock) with the topcoat removed to reveal the dense soft undercoat. If done correctly, the procedure is painless. Many dogs are reported to enjoy having their coats stripped, especially when they are introduced to the process as puppies.

Why do we hand-strip terriers? What is hand-stripping? What skills are needed to be successful at hand-stripping (for both groomer and dog being stripped)?

Hand-stripping is a technique that allows a wirehaired terrier's natural coat to be maintained. By this, we mean maintaining a coat that is virtually dustproof as well as waterproof, while keeping its rich look intact.

With hand-stripping, we are constantly removing the hard outer hair. The soft undercoat provides the insulation and is not removed. One important skill for groomers is understanding and recognizing the difference between the undercoat (the soft hair) and the outer coat, consisting of the wiry hair.

As each animal is a "study of one," we determine, on an individual basis, exactly what each dog is able to tolerate and is comfortable with at any given time.

Of equal importance are patience and observation: patience, as it is a lengthy process, and observation, in order to realize at which point the dog may need to take a break. To ensure the dog's comfort, groomers want to be certain not to pull out too much hair at one time, and to only pull out those hairs that are loose enough to come out easily. It is also important to take care that you are pulling the hair that's ready to come out *in the proper direction*, and to be cognizant of the amount of time you are asking the dog to remain standing still while being handled on the table. We recommend, as always, clicking (or using verbal marker word) and treating throughout the process for the dog's calm behavior.

Remember, all the extra care and time that you as the groomer take with the process is valuable. Most families understand this, and will pay extra for your sensitivity to their dog's needs.

One helpful note here is to be aware that if the dog you're working with is uncomfortable, frightened, or stressed, he may be unable and unwilling to take even high-value treats. In this situation, the dog is now anorexic (unable to eat or accept even high-value treats). If you notice that a dog is not taking treats, it likely means that he is not comfortable and that you should stop and change your plan. In this case, stopping and taking a break is a very powerful reinforcer for the dog, and might be just what is needed for both groomer and dog to be able to comfortably spend a bit more time finishing the job.

Over time, you can build a longer and longer duration that the dog is comfortable with while standing on the table and having the hand-stripping done. The way to arrive at a lengthier duration is by working in short sessions. Another benefit of this is that as you eventually build duration, the time spent stripping a particular dog will speed up considerably, while the price that you have established for the service will remain fixed. Thus, over time, and in the long run, you increase your income.

Let's look at some of the skills needed for this process, and let's also talk about ways to acquire them, from both the dog's and the groomer's perspective.

Hand-stripping is necessary in order to maintain a wire coat; however, it is not necessary for the dog's overall good health. Since it's a type of coat maintenance that is often perceived as uncomfortable (and *is* uncomfortable if not shaped correctly), it is generally reserved for show dogs. For example, in order to be shown, the standard requires wirehaired terriers to be hand-stripped.

Simply put, and generally for all terriers, the process requires pulling out the topcoat and allowing the undercoat to remain. The primary skills of importance for the groomer to have are patience and observation. Patience means going slowly, as has been emphasized in this book; keen observation is key in learning how and what to watch in order to determine what the dog is communicating so that you may know the point at which the dog may need to take a break.

In order to ensure the dog's comfort, groomers want to be certain not to pull out too much hair at one time so as to be sure that they are pulling in the proper direction, and to be cognizant of the amount of time they are asking the dog to remain standing still and being handled on the table.

This is where desensitization and a positive approach are helpful and beneficial. Ideally, in order to gain optimum success, this training would begin when the dog is still a puppy, and way before the animal's first stripping session.

This early training can result in a great way to generate more business via your advertising. It would be helpful to have a section about hand-stripping, describing its benefits and how, in the long run, taking the time to positively shape the dog to remain calm and relaxed during this process will be cost effective for the client. Hand-stripping is being used more and more, so it might be beneficial to the guardian of a new wire-coated dog to have a lesson or two in how to recognize when his or her dog needs to be stripped. In addition, you can teach the guardian, perhaps via a mini-lesson, about how he or she can be of assistance to you the groomer, as well as to the dog, by consistently helping to shape cooperation with the stripping procedure.

Our recommendation is to endeavor to spend as much time as needed for the dog to feel comfortable with a procedure. This extra time will pay off in speediness and relaxation later. Remember to take note that if the animal you're working with is uncomfortable, frightened, or stressed, the dog may also be anorexic. If the dog is anxious, teach the animal that it's perfectly okay for it to withdraw. You have recognized the dog's communication and have identified it as a good time for both you and the dog to take a break.

Signs of stress that indicate the dog would like a break include the animal backing away, mouthing your hand, and/or some of the more subtle cues such as stiffening, panting, or lip licking (see Chapter 3 – Body Language).

Hand-Stripping at Home
We have previously discussed handling techniques, so let's apply them now. Step one would be to have the puppy come in for the Meet and Treat during the socialization period prior to fourteen weeks. The Meet and Treat should be arranged as early as possible for a puppy that's going to need to be groomed on a regular basis so that the grooming shop and the grooming process can be introduced gradually-- a key concept

for all puppies.

Depending on the dog's comfort level, the Meet and Treat may need to be repeated several times.

Step two would be to arrange an in-home session. The goals of this lesson would be to help the guardian to understand that hand-stripping is an ongoing, lifelong process, and to realize that the family's at-home assistance will be invaluable in helping the dog to feel comfortable and relaxed with it.

The lesson would begin with your teaching the guardian how to brush the dog properly. During this session, the guardian would learn how to distinguish the outer coat from the undercoat. This piece of the process is extremely important—and especially vital in the case of hand-stripping. You can also teach the guardian how to begin to help the dog to calmly station in one spot.

We can't stress enough how important it is to teach the animal to voluntarily cooperate in its own care. Currently, in up-to-date AZA-accredited zoos and aquariums, this is the only way that large animals can be medicated, examined, etc.

With this in mind, we want to first desensitize the puppy to having his hair pulled. While this may sound like the "easy" part, the skin is, in fact, the body's largest organ and, as such, contains many, many neurotransmitters, the most sensitive being the ones at the base of each hair follicle that allow the animal to understand its place in its infinity; an example would be the whiskers on a cat that allow it to recognize spatial perception. In consideration of this, we want to start this process very slowly.

Sample training plan: Hand-Stripping
Working from the base of the neck through the withers, to the base of the tail is the easy part, so that's where we'll start our shaping plan.

Have plenty of tiny, soft high-value treats on hand for your session.

1. Pet, palpate and brush the dog all over (something that families should also do on a daily basis). Click and treat for calm behavior. While doing this, note and learn to identify the difference between the hard outer coat and the undercoat.
2. Learn to isolate (not pull) just one hair on the topcoat. Practice to see if you can do that all over the back, being sure to click and treat for any calm behavior. At this stage, we are just touching the hair, isolating it, and clicking/treating for calm/relaxed behavior. We are not yet doing any pulling.

3. Once you are able to isolate the hair, and the dog is able to remain calm, the next step would be to go from the back of the head down the neck again, isolating just one hair at a time. Remember to click and treat for calm behavior.
4. Once the dog is comfortable with being handled, and relaxed while having his hair tugged all over, continue working on this practice daily until you notice that the hair is starting to actually come out. Reminder: Be careful to make sure that you can see the little white root at the end of the hair.
5. The next step is to grab two hairs (and for the following step, you will grab three hairs), all the while clicking and treating for calm behavior. As you are doing this, be sure to note in which direction the hair is growing, as hair grows in many different directions. This is important since, when you ultimately pull, you want to pull in the direction that the hair is growing.
6. The groomer is working on her skills while also desensitizing the dog to remaining in a still, standing position and while allowing tugging all over his coat. Remember, it will be so much easier once the animal is accustomed to the standing/pulling, and the groomer has developed the skill to be able to quickly pull just a few hairs out at a time.
7. Finally, take the time to help the dog to feel comfortable.

Please don't try to do it all in one sitting. Take breaks, and even divide the work up into more than one session when necessary.

Next, try to experiment with the back legs, the tail, the front paws, and the chest. The ears, the belly, and the area around the rectum are all very sensitive areas, so it's very important not only to isolate the hairs by hand, but also to shape the dog to stand still so you can pluck them out individually. When actually pulling the hair out, be sure to use the hand not involved in pulling to stretch the skin in the opposite direction; in this way, the hair will come out easily. Once more, the rationale for using your fingers, and only plucking a few strands at a time, especially in those extra-sensitive areas, is that it is the best way to help desensitize the dog gradually to the process.

An important point to remember here is that you want to pull the hair out so that you are able to see the little white root at the end. This criterion is key in making sure you don't cut the hair. Using your hands and sometimes the use of chalk can be helpful, along with rubber thumbs. Other tools include volcanic rock or pumice stone, and rubber fingertips to grasp the hair.

Learning to strip using these alternative tools has advantages over using stripping knives. Stripping knives are very useful if you know how to use them, but using them incorrectly can result in permanent damage to the dog's coat. The danger lies in ripping out the hair and inadvertently cutting it. Rather, the hair should be carefully braced up against the flat part of the knife which then gives you leverage to pull. The worst thing that you can do is cut through the hair; should that occur, the hair will not grow back the same way. Additionally, you want to take care not to destroy the character of the wiry coat by cutting or pulling too much hair out at a time. To repeat—inadvertently cutting the hair risks ruining the coat!

Keep in mind that you should charge more for stripping. The standard is to bill at an hourly rate as it's a highly skilled job and is very labor-intensive. Also, if done properly, and in such a way that your dog and human client are happy, you can secure a customer for the next fifteen years.

To get started, we recommend rolling the coat at the beginning of this process. This is defined as only pulling out the hair that is ready to come out. This will also translate to more frequent and shorter grooming visits. If you start with a puppy, and set aside a few minutes at different times of the day for the pup to come in and just have his hair lightly combed and pulled all over, this will slowly begin the desensitization process.

You will again find that some parts of the body are much more sensitive than others. For example, the hair between the eyes at the point where the nose and the top meet is a highly sensitive spot. You will find the same level of increased sensitivity around the rectum, the genitals, the ears, the flanks, and the belly, so you will want to spend a bit more time and take things a little more slowly in these areas.

Oftentimes, you will find groomers "faking" these spots (using a thinning shears); however, it is possible to desensitize to the pulling in these locations as well. In order to do so, the suggestion is to focus on these specific body locations by learning to hold the skin tighter than you would in another area, and pulling just a few hairs out at a time. You may even pull just one hair out at a time. By going this route, you will ultimately get the animal really comfortable with the process, and the overall look of the coat will be magnificent.

12 SPECIALTY DOGS: Contest Dogs

Every contest/competition dog can develop a special bond with its groomer. This is true whether it's the groomer's own dog or a client's dog.

Photo credit: Anne Francis

For the groomer, a dog that has been previously shown in the breed ring is ideal to work with since the dog has often been trained for hours of grooming. A quality-bred puppy is also a delight. Quality breeders will have already started getting their pups used to the sounds and motions of grooming. Getting a quality-bred puppy or adult dog for yourself, or if you are lucky enough to have a client come through your door with one, will provide you with the opportunity to groom these potential or seasoned competition dogs.

Competition grooming goes above and beyond what is expected of a pet during regular grooming. Contest dogs are bathed and blow-dried at least once a week (not hand-stripped terriers, but they get pulled on). Sometimes these wash-and-dry sessions are even more frequent if the dog is going through a coat change or if the groomer is using a lot of products on the coat. Dogs also get their nails trimmed or filed, ears cleaned, and pads clipped on a regular basis.

When considering a contest dog, it is important to be honest with yourself and/or the dog's family about the commitment you will be making. This is a labor of love requiring lots of time and energy. Aside from the grooming aspect, the dog needs to be a good traveler, crate-trained, enjoy long car rides, and be able to be quiet when left alone in hotel rooms. These are all considered "musts" when competing.

For starters, appropriately crate-training all dogs in general is always recommended, as you never know when an emergency could arise and a crate is needed. Also, crates are the safest way to travel with a dog in the car. Too, when you are not present, we advise leaving dogs crated in a hotel room for safety's sake; a maid could open the door at any time, frightening the dog or allowing the dog to escape.

Contest dogs should be well-socialized and able to walk in crowded areas without pulling, jumping, or causing any type of commotion. With their coats and behavior, they should be breed ambassadors. We want them to represent well in public places such as hotels, rest areas, airports, etc., and to be comfortable and on their best behavior.

With both our own contest dogs and clients' contest dogs, we recommend starting by having them on the grooming table regularly. Once they are comfortable there, we give them a bed on the table and a "chew" or food puzzle, and just let them "hang out." They might practice this stationing behavior by staying on another grooming table right next to yours while you are working on another dog. This also helps them learn to ignore dogs on other tables, dogs and people walking by, and other potentially distracting sounds. The food puzzle or chew also helps to create a positive association with the experience.

The next skill we need to teach is to "stack." To stack a dog means to have the dog stand in a way that shows his best virtues by standing squarely on the table. Stacking is the art of presenting the dog in such a way as to show off his best features and to demonstrate how the dog will look while doing his job.

Photo credit: Anne Francis

Another helpful part of this process is to acclimate the dog to the contest venue. You can practice this type of interaction by asking some friends and co-workers to come by to greet the dog, run their hands over the dog, pick his feet up, and/or comb hands through his hair while he stands calmly in place. This helps the dog to experience and desensitize to what a judge will do. We recommend treating for calm behavior at each step of this process. Too, if the dog becomes uncomfortable or startled or stressed, just pause briefly and then make it "easier" via a shorter time on the table, less people passing by, and less frequent touching. Then you can eventually build back up to more contact/people/etc.

All these behaviors are learned over time and, as mentioned, are accompanied by treating and praise, which help the dog to create positive associations with these behaviors and situations.

Becoming a competition dog and all that goes along with this job should be fun for the dogs; we want them to enjoy and look forward to the experience. However, not every dog will want to be a model! The dogs that excel in this type of work will enjoy the one-on-one undivided attention they get from the professional groomer.

Another bonus for contest dogs is that, in many ways, going to the shows offers opportunities to get to do things that are not necessarily allowed at home, like sleeping on the bed, special treats in the crates while traveling, or just having social interaction with other dogs (some of them being "only" dogs at home). These "extras" may be very reinforcing for the dog who is well suited to the contest dog life.

13 FINDING QUALITY PROFESSIONAL GROOMERS AND TRAINERS

Finding a Quality Professional Groomer

Sometimes it can be a challenge to uncover what constitutes a quality groomer and/or grooming shop. You can start off with word-of-mouth—information from people that you meet or see in the park or on the street with dogs that have nice haircuts.

Photo credit: Chelsea Dasso Hamlin

All grooming shops should be licensed by the local Department of Health. While Internet reviews should be taken

...ith a grain of salt, you can get a general sense of where to begin based upon reviews.

See if the shop offers a "Meet and Treat" (i.e., that *practice*; the term itself may not be familiar to everyone). If so, use that opportunity wisely to ask a lot of questions of the shop owner and/or groomer (if the owner isn't one and the same) while assessing whether the shop is clean. Grooming shops have dirty dogs traipsing in all the time, so while we want to be sure the shop doesn't have a bad smell, some dog odors will be reasonable.

You should inquire about things like how long the dog would be expected to stay, and what their policy is if the dog becomes stressed— if the groomers are encouraged to allow an animal to take breaks, or if they just continue working in order to get the job done.

You can also inquire as to how long the shop has been in business. You might even want to call the local Department of Health to see if the shop is up-to-date on its records, and whether or not it has or has had any outstanding violations or summonses at the moment or in the past.

Finally, as grooming is currently a largely unregulated field, it will be important to ask if the groomers participate in continuing education or have earned any certifications.

Another role that groomers play is observing, noting, and providing feedback to their human clients about their dogs and their dog's behavior. Frequently you may find that you come across a dog that has behavioral issues, and that certainly could use some professional help. Professional help with reactivity, fear, and general training can go a long way toward a calmer, smoother, and safer grooming appointment.

Finding a Quality Professional Trainer

Unfortunately, dog training (as with dog grooming) is currently an unregulated field. As such, for the best outcomes, you want to be certain to make an informed decision about who would be an effective dog-training candidate for your pup and your household.

Specifically, you want to ensure that you work with a professional who uses positive reinforcement and is educated in training methods that are based on the science of applied behavioral analysis (ABA). When choosing a dog trainer, it is important to do your research to avoid being misled by the latest buzzwords or fancy-sounding terminology.

Your pet-training specialist should be professional and

proficient at working with animals as well as people in a considerate and compassionate manner.

Two of the most well-known and respected dog training programs are The Academy of Dog Trainers and the Karen Pryor Academy. You should ask the trainers you are considering about their professional backgrounds, and if they are certified as having passed both knowledge-based and practical standards.

Photo credit: Brad Waggoner

Moreover, the Certification Council for Professional Dog Trainers is a professional organization and an independent certification body. For a dog trainer to be certified by them they must pass a rigorous evaluation exam. Typically, trainers who have met their requirements will use the designation: Certified Professional Dog Trainer, Knowledge Assessed (CPDT-KA).

Professionals should also have credentials whereby they are required to accumulate continuing educational credits in order to maintain their certification. This helps to ensure that professionals stay current with the latest science-based information and methodologies.

Dog trainers with the above-mentioned accreditation/credentials will welcome your questions. Specifically, you want to ask any potential trainers you might work with how they train—what methods and/or type of training they use. Reward-based trainers will likely use several positive approaches and/or suggestions in order to modify a behavior, and will always seek to reinforce behaviors that they like, while ignoring (not giving attention to) those that they don't wish to see continue.

Reward-based trainers will want to instruct dog families on how to have alternative behaviors replace the behaviors they don't wish to see continue by using treats, play, affection, and attention to reinforce behaviors that they want their dogs to repeat.

Your trainer should recognize that relationships, for both people and animals, are built on trust and, as such, should utilize modern, scientific methods to train and interact with.

Be sure that the trainer is a good communicator with the dogs and the people he or she is working with, along with being available for questions and individual assistance as needed. The dog-training instructor should be supportive and encouraging and have a genuine interest in what she is doing. Too, she should engage professionally and positively with both canine and human clients.

14 WORKING WITH PEOPLE

When discussing working with animals, we cannot exclude the fact that we are also working with people. Risë Van Fleet has a great resource entitled, "The Human Half of Dog Training" (2012). While this reference is aimed at animal trainers, the interpersonal interactions are a key component for groomers, and the skills discussed are very transferable to the work and world of dog grooming. Too, it is important to understand and recognize the boundaries of your knowledge base, and to know when to seek the help of a qualified and professional force-free trainer.

Photo credit: Alice Tong

As discussed earlier, there will be many times when you as the groomer will need to encourage the animal's caregivers to work on some skills at home and outside of the grooming shop. Encouraging families to collaborate in this way will help make the grooming experience exponentially less stressful for their dog.

There may be other times when you will need to help the owner realize and balance expectations with what is in the best interests of the animal at the moment. For example, if the dog arrives in an extreme state of stress, you may need to communicate to the family that for the welfare of the animal, right now, at least, you might have to break the grooming tasks down into more than one appointment. As for the future visits that will need to take place throughout the dog's lifetime, whether or not to employ this gradual process will be contingent on the dog's stress levels at those times.

Another technique that could prove helpful in working with the human half of your clientele is TAG teaching. TAG stands for teaching with acoustical guidance. Per Theresa McKeon and Joan Orr via Tagteach.com:

> What is the point? With TAGteach™, a revolutionary new way of teaching, it's a tag point. The tag point is the specific learning goal that the teacher will mark with a tag that highlights success for the learner. The tag pinpoints the exact moment the tag point is executed correctly and gives immediate and clear feedback to the learner.

TAG is yet another skill that can aid in communicating with clients (the human portion) to enable them to better understand exactly which skill sets we are attempting to pinpoint. A few examples might be as follows:

- Tag point for guardians: Check daily for tangles and mats.
- Tag point for guardians: Comb out one body part a day.
- Tag points for guardians: Notice mat forming; contact groomer.
- Tag point for groomers: Communicate with clients regularly.
- Tag point for groomers: Explain about areas that mat.
- Tag point for groomers: Explain how to prevent mats forming.

As a professional, it is your responsibility to learn and understand the skills associated with grooming, to have knowledge about behavioral science, and to read and react appropriately to the non-verbal communication and body language of your animal clients.

Positive reinforcement is now being used everywhere, and going viral! The scientific data is in—and it works—so why not get on board!

Fishermen on big processing ships in the Bering Sea who, in the past, have been berated and abused in their training in order to get results, are now learning the skills needed to perform their jobs by each skill being broken down and reinforced.

We are also seeing the influence of positive reinforcement in the education of doctors and surgeons who, in the past, have been bullied into performance. These same professionals are now being trained more efficiently and to a higher level of excellence via positive reinforcement.

Athletes, dancers, and golfers are a few more adherents of the disciplines where positive reinforcement is spreading and seeing great success!

Let's include the grooming industry in the professions that are seeing more and more success using positive reinforcement for greater results.

This book provides recipes that will help you to hone your shaping skills in a way that enables your dog clients to enjoy the experience. With a little extra effort, we can enhance our relationships and improve our work skills and experiences while staying safer and earning more in the way of client retention and income!

Groomers, you have spent a great deal of time, money, and energy on your skills. You are committed to continuing education via videos, conferences, and expos, as well as keeping informed about trends via trade magazines and articles, etc. As such, you will want to be certain that you are appropriately compensated for your work. Using the most modern skills and techniques to assure that your clients are relaxed and comfortable in your work together means that you deserve the top recompense available.

It is helpful to keep in mind that your clients are both the dogs and the humans. Focusing on building both relationships is key in helping to steer you in the right direction and set you up for success as you forge a positive long-term relationship with the dogs in your care and the people who make up their families.

On a final note, our inspiration for promoting an increased understanding of force-free handling techniques in the grooming field comes from our desire to enhance the modern groomer's perspective for effective empathetic, gentle, collaborative, and voluntary methods. Additionally, we hope that this guide may inspire groomers in their continuing efforts to incorporate the least invasive techniques, an endeavor that will prove invaluable in building and maintaining long-lasting relationships in their practices. Finally, via the use of low-stress techniques, groomers will contribute greatly to the industry's development, and assume leadership roles in individual grooming businesses across the industry.

We seek to have this book become a resource for groomers in their efforts to educate families in the ever-evolving positive-reinforcement approaches to comprehensive care—which includes relaxed, safe, and comfortable grooming visits.

REFERENCES

Donaldson, Jean. (2002). (n.p.). *Mine*. Dogwise Publishing. Print.

Michaels, Linda, MA (n.d.). "If Your Dog Could Talk: Reward vs Punishment Dog Training." Retrieved from https://positively.com/contribuors/if-your-dog-could-talk-reward-vs-punishment-dog-training. Originally published in *Natural Awakenings Pet Magazine. (*n.d.)

Stilwell, Victoria. (n.d.)."Being Nice to Your Dog is Good Science." Retrieved from https://positively.com/contributors/being-nice-to-your-dog-is-good-science/

Pryor, Karen. "The Modern Principles of Shaping." *Better Together: The Collected Wisdom of Modern Dog Trainers*, edited by Ken Ramirez, Sunshine Books, Inc., 2017, p. 51.

Rossman, Randi. (2014). "Dog Training 101: Respondent (Classical) Conditioning, and Counter Conditioning." [Blog post] The Dog Guy. Retrieved from https://dogguy.net/2014/09/16/dog-training-101-respondent-classical-conditioning-and-counter-conditioning/. Originally posted on the Fearful Dogs Facebook page.

Stilwell, Victoria. (n.d.) "Flooding." Retrieved from https://positively.com/dog-training/positive-training/victoria-stilwell-articles/flooding. para. 4.

van Fleet, Risë. *The Human Half of Dog Training.* Dogwise Publishing, 2012.